# The
# Killer Storms
Hurricanes, Typhoons, and Tornadoes

## GARY JENNINGS

J. B. LIPPINCOTT COMPANY
Philadelphia    New York

For Francesca
*who came with me through a hurricane*

ERRATUM

The illustrations on pages 57 and 185 of this book
have unfortunately been transposed. The picture on
page 57 belongs with the caption on page 185 and the
picture on 185 belongs with the caption on page 57.
The publisher apologizes to the reader for this error.

*The Killer Storms* by Gary Jennings

J. B. Lippincott Company

# ACKNOWLEDGMENTS

For information, advice, research assistance, the loan of photographs, and numerous other kinds of help, this book and I are indebted to Mr. Herbert S. Lieb of the Environmental Science Services Administration; Lieutenant Colonel Gerald W. Holland of the U.S. Air Force; Major General Joseph D. ("Smokey") Caldara, USAF (Ret.); Mr. Roy S. Popkin and Mr. Edwin H. Powers of the American National Red Cross; Mrs. Marne Martin; Brigadier Andrew S. Miller of the Salvation Army (USA); *Teniente Coronel* Harlan M. Cleveland of the Salvation Army (Mexico); Mr. Mart P. Bushnell of the Boy Scouts of America; Mrs. Betty Shepard and Miss Judith Gaylor of the Girl Scouts of the USA; the kindly librarians and Miss Garnetta Kramer, Director, of the *Biblioteca* Benjamin Franklin, Mexico City; Mr. Victor Avers of Radio WRAD, whose voluminous and eclectic news files provided some of the more arcane weather anecdotes and oddities; and especially to my brother, Mr. Hiram Jennings, who singlehandedly unearthed the bones of Last Island.

G. J.

# CONTENTS

# THE KILLER STORMS

# 1
# HURAKÁN

The islands known today as the West Indies are probably the nearest thing to paradise that man has found on this earth.

The first explorers to find them—before history began—were the brown-skinned tribes called Taíno, Lucayo, and Igneri, who originally lived along the northern coasts of the South American continent. These were gentle people, and their life on the mainland had been made intolerable by more warlike neighbors, the Caribs, who continually preyed upon them. Preferring flight to fight, the beleaguered people ventured out to sea in canoes—one party after another over the years—and beyond the horizon they found a haven in these islands.

Many later visitors have compared the West Indies to "emeralds set in a sea of sapphires." But really there is nothing about the islands so hard or cold or sharp as jewels. Everything is soft and warm and mild: the gentle seas, the murmuring breezes, the talcum-powder sand of their beaches. From a distance the islands are "emerald" indeed, covered with a profusion of green growing things.

But up close the green is often hard to see among the other gemlike colors—ruby red, topaz yellow, amethyst purple—of the flamboyant flowers and birds that flourish everywhere.

The newly arrived tribesmen were delighted to discover that here a man didn't have to labor just to live. When he got hungry he could catch himself a meal of seafood, or he could pluck fruits growing wild. In this balmy climate a house needn't be more than a flimsy shelter; palm trees provided trunks for the uprights and fronds for the roof thatch. A man didn't even have to wear a scrap of clothing, unless for modesty's sake or the pride of ornamentation. For this there were abundant palm leaves, the feathers of birds, and trinkets of seashells.

The newcomers were thankful for this paradise they'd found, and they were dutiful about saying "thank you" to the various gods they believed responsible for their good luck. Like most primitive peoples, these tribesmen did not recognize one single, all-powerful god, but saw a separate spirit in every different aspect of nature. There might be one god of flowers, another of trees, another of fruits, a god of the sun, and a god of the sea. The islanders thanked them all for the bounty they had bestowed—and continued to pray and offer sacrifices so the gods would go on giving their blessings.

For example, even in paradise some rain must fall. When the islands began to be parched after a season of uninterrupted sunshine, the people would appeal to their rain god, and in due course would come the refreshing showers. Sometimes, though, these came with thunder and lightning, not so welcome as the simple rain. So the people had a separate storm god, too, and to him they prayed *not* to send his blessings.

Nevertheless, almost every year there came at least one storm that was worse than all the other storms put together. Its black clouds and deluge of rain rode a wind like a battering-ram, a wind that no man, no palm-leaf hut, and sometimes not even the sturdiest trees could stand against. The most awful thing about this particular storm was that it seldom struck just once and then moved on. Often it was two disasters rolled into one.

Its first murderous onslaught might last for hours or a day or more, then there would be a pause as if the storm was gathering its breath. But in a matter of minutes, or an hour, or a few hours at the most, the storm would strike again just as fiercely as before— only now from the opposite direction. The few huts that had stood fast during the storm's first pass could seldom survive this second smashing blow from their other flank.

The islanders already had their rain god to thank for life-giving showers. And they had their storm god to blame for thunderbolts and cloudbursts. But this one distinctive kind of storm was so exceptionally devastating that they thought it simply must have a separate god of its own, and him they beseeched with their most heartfelt fervor *please* to stay away.

To this dread god the islanders gave the name of HURAKÁN.

# 2
# HURRICANE!

Today we know that this killer storm is not really the work of any bad-tempered god. We know that it is simply a vast, churning circle of winds—like a merry-go-round gone wild—roaring around a central area (the "eye") that is comparatively calm and still. Like a merry-go-round mounted on a truck, the storm travels in a forward direction at the same time that it is fiercely whirling. First the leading edge of the spinning storm sweeps over a ground area, then the calm eye, then the storm's trailing edge. Thus, although the storm essentially consists of just one circling wind, it *does* strike twice from opposite directions.

The storm is not really a "killer" in the sense that it destroys deliberately or has any ill will of its own. The storm develops from the natural interactions of heat, air, moisture, and the rotation of the earth, and so it is no more a monstrosity than sunshine or the seasons. But it is the most powerful and destructive force that has ever been unleashed on our world. Compared to the energy let loose in just one such storm, other natural upheavals like volcanoes and

*Hurricane coming! A U.S. Coast Guard station hoists the internationally recognized warning flags—two of them, bright red with a square black center.*

ESSA

earthquakes, or man-made devastations like a hydrogen-bomb explosion, are comparative pipsqueaks. So, although this kind of weather disturbance is an entirely natural phenomenon of nature, "killer storm" remains an accurate epithet for it.

The killer storm still bedevils us, just as it did the earliest inhabitants of the West Indies, and we might say that the dread god does, too, since our word "hurricane" derives from his name. *Hurakán* was one of the first native words that the white man learned when he arrived in the New World, because the storm was the first and worst danger he encountered here.

It's a minor miracle that the earliest and most famous of all the white explorers ever arrived safely in these islands, or got safely back to Europe to announce his discovery. It was August, the very peak of the "hurricane season," when Christopher Columbus set out from Spain on his initial voyage in 1492, and he set his course for that part of the Atlantic Ocean where the hurricanes blow the worst. Of course, Columbus did not know that hurricanes existed. But it may be that he had a brush with one of these mighty storms without even realizing it.

At one point in mid-ocean, his three tiny ships were tossed and rocked by a heavy sea swell. These waves were something new in the sailors' experience, because there was no accompanying high wind to account for them. Almost certainly they were the evidence of a hurricane raging somewhere far over the horizon, because such a storm can send billows surging thousands of miles across the sea.

These oddly windless waves were a puzzle, but no hazard, and eventually the explorers made landfall in those islands known today as the Bahamas. During the remainder of that first exploration of the New World, the adventurers never felt any other touch of a hurricane. On the return trip to Spain, early in 1493, they endured no storm worse than the Atlantic's winter gales.

During his later voyages to the West Indies, Columbus did encounter full-blown hurricanes, and confessed his terror of them. After one violent storm had sunk three of his ships, he remarked that, except for his desire to serve God and king—by finding new lands in which to plant the Christian religion and the flag of Spain—*nothing* would induce him to expose himself to such dangers as the wrath of the hurricane.

Other seafarers fanning out from Europe into other alien seas also found devastating storms and, if they survived, they learned the native names for them. Around the Gulf of Arabia, for instance, the most dreaded storm was the *asifa-t*. The fiercest storm of the North Pacific was known to the Chinese as the *ty-fung,* meaning "great wind" (the European sailors found it easier to say "tuffoon" or "typhoon"). In the Philippine Islands the same storm was called the *baguio,* and in Japan the *reppu.* The first white settlers of Australia copied a native word and called the worst of their coastal storms the "willy-willy." On the other side of the Pacific, along the western seaboard of Mexico and Central America, the Spanish colonists called the storm the *cordonazo.*

Although these great storms have long had different names, and are found in widely scattered areas, all of them are really the same kind of weather disturbance—identical to the hurricane—with only minor variations according to the part of the world that it occurs in. Since the people of each area still call "their" storm by its local name, a single such storm may be variously described as a *baguio,* a *ty-fung* and a *reppu,* as it roars past the Philippines, the China coast and then the islands of Japan. However, most professional weathermen today use only two of the old-time names. If the storm takes place anywhere in the western hemisphere, it is called a hurricane; in the Far East it's a typhoon.

By whatever name it is known, this worst of all the earth's storms can be more than an immediate disaster in one particular locality; it can have wide-ranging effects on people and events far removed from its area of activity. We realize, now, that the success of Columbus' first expedition, and his discovery of the New World, resulted from the absence of any interfering hurricane. But more often the *presence* of such a storm has drastically changed the course of human history.

During the great Age of Exploration that followed Columbus' trail-blazing voyages, the far-wandering seafarers brought back to Europe horrendous tales of the storms they had survived in foreign seas, and made words like "typhoon" and "willy-willy" familiar. But the storm and the name that became best known was "hurricane"—simply because it was encountered the most often by European sailors.

With the opening up of the New World, many more ships went there than to any other corner of the earth. Spanish, Portuguese, French, Dutch, and English explorers scouted the coasts of both North and South America. The Spanish conquistadors forged inland, wresting vast territories from the natives. Treasure-hunters came, and missionaries bringing Christianity to the heathen. Colonists came to settle and to work the land. Pirates came, to prey on the merchant ships and to plunder the young port cities. For some two centuries after Columbus, most of this sea traffic and land settlement was concentrated among the islands of the West Indies and around the Gulf of Mexico coast from Yucatán to Florida. This is the area of the worst hurricanes.

*The first blasting wind of an approaching hurricane whips the palm trees and lashes the sea into white spume along a Florida coast.*

ESSA

The white men, from the very beginning of their migration to the New World, suffered far more from hurricanes than the natives ever had. During the Indians' undisturbed occupancy of these lands, it is probable that hurricanes killed no more than a few individuals each year. They had learned how to recognize the storm's approach, to respect its terrible strength, and to take shelter. Furthermore, their houses were only huts; if the hurricane demolished these buildings, they could be rebuilt immediately from the materials right at hand. Their sea craft were canoes hollowed out of fallen tree trunks; if they sank they were easily raised, if blown out to sea they were easily replaced.

By contrast, each newly arriving shipload of Europeans came with no experience of such storms, no knowledge of how to cope with them and, worst, no sensible fear of them. Even when the friendly Indians warned the newcomers that a hurricane was approaching, and tried to describe what it would be like, the new arrivals were inclined to scoff at such "tall tales" and unmanly fears. Until a man has actually endured a hurricane, it's hard for him to believe that there *can* be such an upheaval of nature.

Even when the white man managed to save his own skin, he stood to lose other things. His ships, compared to the Indians' craft, were immense, ponderous, and complicated machines. When they sank they were almost impossible to raise, even from shallow water. When they were smashed against a reef, they were not easily repaired. When they were grounded on a sandbar or tossed high and dry onto a beach, they were not easily refloated.

And the colonists who arrived to establish permanent settlements were often unwise about the location of them. For the convenience of shipping, they built their towns right at the shore line. Or, for defense against attack, they built on a hilltop. The seaside settlements were in easy reach of the storm waves, and the hill towns were wide open to the storm winds. Also, the colonists built European-style houses of solid wood and masonry. These were seldom solid enough to withstand a hurricane and, when such a building was blown to pieces, its stones and timbers became flying missiles of death and destruction.

The first "European" town in the western hemisphere—the settlement which Columbus founded on the island of Hispaniola during his second voyage, and named for his patron queen, Isabella—lasted only a short time before it was wiped out by a hurricane. There were many other such towns, brand-new and ambitious, that similarly vanished from the map, and there was scarcely a one that escaped *some* damage from the killer storms. But the New World was worth the risk. It was a treasure-house of priceless minerals, new and exotic foodstuffs, free and fertile lands, Indian slaves for the taking—so the white man persisted in his determination to put down roots here.

The Spanish, who had discovered the new continents of North and South America, plundered and exploited them for a century with no rivals to contest their claims. But they did suffer the devastations of the hurricane. Many a ship that set out from Spain disappeared before it ever saw the New World. Other ships arrived in America to find that the port of destination had disappeared. And to this day the sea bottom between America and Europe is littered with untold riches of gold, silver, and precious stones, spilled from the cargo ships that perished when they met a hurricane on their way home.

During Columbus' fourth visit to America, in 1503, he was in the island port of Santo Domingo when one of the first of Spain's treasure fleets was preparing to sail homeward with a cargo of Indian slaves and gold. Columbus knew something about hurricanes by now, and he had detected signs of one blowing up. He cautioned the convoy's commander to postpone departure and stay in the sheltered lee of the island—as he and his own ships were going to do—until after the storm danger had passed. But the commander, a haughty and stubborn man, refused to heed the warning.

The flotilla sailed and, two days later, twenty of its twenty-four ships ended their voyage inside the boiling cauldron of a hurricane,

going to the bottom with their crews of five hundred sailors, an unknown number of Indians, and their cargoes of incalculable value.
Three of the fleet's vessels managed to get back to the island. Only
one ship of that ill-fated flotilla plowed through the hurricane and
on to Spain.

Between the time of America's discovery and the end of the
seventeenth century, a total of more than 150 treasure-laden
Spanish vessels were lost to the killer storms. But there were always
other seafarers, fortune-hunters, and adventurers who were willing
to brave the dangers. So Spain replaced the lost ships with new
and stronger merchant vessels, built fighting ships to protect them
against pirates, and sent ever more and larger fleets into the
American waters.

Although Spain built these ships for the specific purpose of trade
with its New World colonies—and built the ships strong and
heavy in the hope of their withstanding the Atlantic storms—
the result was that, by the mid-1500's, Spain had the most powerful
navy and the biggest merchant fleet in the world. In a very real
sense, it was the hurricane that had inspired Spain to become
"master of the seas."

Spain's emergence as a sea power alarmed the people of England. Because England is an island, the sea was its "castle moat,"
its protection against attack—so long as English ships dominated
that sea. And the only way England could expand its dominion
was by conquering other nations overseas and settling new colonies
there—another reason for wanting unchallenged access to the
oceans. The two nations were bound to clash eventually in a fight
for supremacy at sea and, when it happened, it was a hurricane
that forced the showdown.

In 1568, nine English merchant ships were caught by a hurricane
in the Gulf of Mexico, and fled before the storm to seek the shelter
of a harbor. They found it in the Mexican port of San Juan de
Ulloa. The ships were still there, repairing their damages after the
storm had passed, when a Spanish fleet sailed into the harbor. The

English captain sent a message to the Spanish flagship, apologizing for trespassing in Spanish waters. He explained that he had had to take refuge in an emergency, and requested the courtesy of Spanish hospitality only until he could put to sea again. But the Spanish commander chose to take the intrusion as an intentional invasion, and opened fire on the English ships. He sank or captured seven of them. Two escaped, to report the incident in England.

From then on, the two nations were enemies and England feverishly set about expanding and arming its fleet to match Spain's. For twenty years, the only battles between the two kingdoms consisted of occasional encounters at sea. Individual English and Spanish warships would cross paths in mid-ocean, and fight until one of them was captured or fled. But by 1588 the built-up English Navy was winning most of these encounters, and the Spanish king Philip II realized that England's new sea power must be destroyed before it got any stronger.

He dispatched the mightiest naval force in the world's history— the "Invincible Armada." It consisted of 130 of Spain's biggest and best-armed warships, and carried a force of 30,000 fighting men. Its orders were to sail through the Bay of Biscay and up the English Channel, sweeping the waters clean of every English ship it met. Then the Armada was to stop at Flanders, pick up an army of Spanish soldiers waiting there, and convoy them across the Channel to invade and conquer England.

The plan might have worked, and England might have been reduced to just another Spanish colony, except that the Invincible Armada was *not* invincible against the hurricane. At this point, not one but two of the killer storms intervened in the course of history.

The Armada intended to take England by surprise, and its planned route of attack was still a well-kept "military secret" when it sailed from Lisbon in May of 1588. But an equally unobserved hurricane, after a furious career in the Americas, came churning across the Atlantic on a collision course with the Armada. The hurricane was old and dying by the time it reached Europe, but it still was strong enough to wreak considerable damage among the war fleet. The entire flotilla had to put into the Spanish port of La Coruña, while its numerous crippled ships were patched up, and thereby lost the chance for a sneak attack on England.

Before the invasion fleet could get under way again, news of its whereabouts had reached England, and that country hastily mustered a defensive force of its own war craft. The Armada sailed into the Channel to find its way barred, and itself out-numbered, by 190 English ships. The Armada might still have accomplished the invasion—because the English vessels were all smaller and less heavily armed than those of the Spanish fleet—and indeed, after ten days of battle, the Armada had fought its way through the defensive screen and into sight of the English coast. But that ten days' delay had lost the war for Spain. For on the night of August 8, 1588, the end of a second hurricane, which had managed to cross the Atlantic without spending all of its destructive power, arrived at the scene of battle.

The English ships were near their own shores, and could put into port to escape the storm. The Spanish had nowhere to shelter. The Armada's ships were scattered, many of them sunk, others wrecked or stranded on beaches all the way up the Channel— several were driven around the north end of the British Isles, not to make landfall until they reached Ireland. Only about half of the Armada's ships and men ever saw Spain again.

To commemorate England's narrow escape from invasion and conquest, Queen Elizabeth ordered that a victory medal be de-signed and struck off. The medal's inscription said simply, "God breathed, and they were scattered."

With that defeat, Spain was finished as a naval power, and England won the title of "master of the seas." The most important consequence was that Spain lost its unrivalled domination of the New World. Spain was no longer able to monopolize the trade routes to America, and its colonial expansion in those continents was at an end. Had it not been for the Armada's collapse—and the hurricanes' part in collapsing it—North America today might be, like South America, largely of Spanish heritage, culture, and language. However, once the Atlantic sea lanes were again open to competition, other countries—notably England and France— began to send increasing numbers of explorers and colonists to the yet unsettled areas of the New World, those lands which eventually became the United States and Canada.

Some of these later settlements, too, were affected by hurricanes to a degree that has affected America's history. After England's first successful New World colony had taken root on the coast of Virginia, subsequent shiploads of other settlers set out for that colony. When the Pilgrims sailed in the *Mayflower,* seeking a new land where they could practice their religion without persecution, Virginia was their destination. But the *Mayflower* went astray.

In mid-Atlantic it encountered a violent storm, almost certainly the fringe of a hurricane. The ship survived the turmoil, but came out of it far off course. Some historians believe that the storm alone was to blame for the *Mayflower's* missing Virginia. Others suggest that the ship's commander, for reasons of his own, deliberately misplaced the Pilgrims and merely used the storm as his excuse. In either case, the storm played *some* part in landing the Pilgrims away north of Virginia, on the bleak capes of Massachusetts, and thereby establishing the second successful English colony on the American seaboard.

It is understandable that mankind's destiny could have been so often affected by the interference of hurricanes when the world's exploration, settlement, commerce, and warfare depended so heavily on wooden ships under canvas sails. But the same storms have equally affected the course of history in more modern times, when ships began to be built of sturdy metal and powered with mechanical engines.

In 1889, when the navy of every leading nation consisted of steam-driven, armor-plated warships, a Pacific typhoon proved that such dreadnaughts were still no more than toys compared to its own destructive power. At the same time, this storm stopped a war in the making.

In the 1880's Germany was attempting to expand its empire by annexing new colonies; one of the places Germany wanted was the island group of Samoa in the South Pacific, strategically situated midway between Hawaii and Australia. The Samoans were unwilling to give up their independence, so Germany sent three warships into the islands' harbor of Apia as a threatening "show of force." When the Samoans still refused to yield, the warships bombarded a native village on shore.

Because there were numerous Americans living in Samoa, the United States dispatched three warships of its own to protect its citizens' lives and property. On March 16, 1889, the American and German naval squadrons confronted each other in Apia harbor. If either side had made the slightest bellicose move at that point, the "Open fire!" order would have been given, and the resulting battle could only have led to a full-scale war between Germany and the United States. However, before any overt actions were made by the combatants, a typhoon crashed down on the islands.

All six of the ships were hurled onto the island reefs, some of them dashed to pieces against the rocks, others stranded helplessly, still others sunk in the tumult of waters—and 150 of the sailors lost their lives. The storm proved to be a common enemy for the Germans and the Americans—and the Samoan islanders as well— so all three factions united as allies to struggle against it. German crewmen washed overboard were plucked from the sea by American lifeboats. German ships threw towlines to haul American vessels off the murderous reefs. The Samoan villagers rescued the castaways of both navies who tumbled ashore half-drowned in the thundering breakers.

Thanks to the typhoon, the almost-war was ended before it began. Instead of deciding Samoa's future at gunpoint, Germany and the United States settled it peaceably—over a conference table later that year—when they and other major world powers agreed that the island group was to remain independent under its own rulers, a neutral territory not to be claimed by any other nation.

One other result of the Samoa incident was the United States' increasing realization that it had "come of age" as a major power—that it now ranked beside the most respected nations of the Old World, and shared their responsibility for helping keep the peace in all parts of the planet. To do its part in curbing warlike aggressors, the United States needed a larger navy, so it began to build new fighting ships. In short, that historic storm contributed to the founding of the modern United States Navy.

That proud navy has not endured many defeats since its formation. One of the few really terrible trouncings it ever suffered was inflicted by still another typhoon. It happened in December of 1944, toward the end of World War II, when the Allied forces were in the process of retaking the Philippine Islands from the Japanese troops who had invaded them early in the war. The Allies had secured possession of several of the smaller southern islands. Now they planned to mount their major assault on the Philippines' main island of Luzon, and in preparation for the landing the Allies were "softening up" the Japanese occupation forces with an intensive air and artillery bombardment by the U.S. Navy's Third Fleet.

After one of its strikes against the Japanese fortifications on Luzon, the Third Fleet withdrew a few hundred miles into the open ocean to rendezvous with tanker ships and refuel for the next foray. But the fleet was caught in mid-Pacific, in the middle of the fueling procedure, by a typhoon that had blown up unnoticed by the Navy weathermen.

Taken by surprise, with many of the ships still too low on fuel to outrun the storm, the fleet milled about in confusion. First it tried to maintain some kind of orderly formation, so that any vessel in distress would have help close at hand. When it became apparent that this tactic only added the danger of ships' ramming into each other, the fleet separated, every vessel for itself, to ride out the storm as best it might.

Three destroyers sank without a trace. Thirteen craft were so severely damaged that they could barely limp back to an Allied port for repairs. Eight other vessels suffered less crippling injuries. The fleet's aircraft carriers lost 146 of their warplanes, either washed off the flight decks or battered into junk. The various ships lost a total of 763 men, either killed on board or vanished overside never to be seen again, and eighty other men were seriously injured.

All in all, it was a worse "defeat" than the Japanese Navy had been able to inflict on the U.S. Navy during the long campaign of fighting for the Philippines. It was fully three weeks before the Third Fleet was capable of combat again—three weeks during which further sea strikes against the Japanese in the Philippines had to be suspended—and without the bombardments the planned invasion of Luzon had to be postponed until early January of 1945.

The typhoon did not, of course, lose the war for the Allies, as the historic storms of 1588 lost that war for Spain. But the 1944 storm *did* temporarily bring to a standstill the world's most modern and efficient fighting machine. The engine-powered steel vessels of the Third Fleet were almost as helpless in that storm as if they had been the Armada's sail-borne wooden galleons. For all our modern technology, we still cannot build a vessel for sea or air travel that can be *guaranteed* secure against the fury of a typhoon or hurricane. So long as so much of our civilization depends on transport and communication across the skies and oceans, the course of world history will still be steered occasionally by the capricious whims of the killer storm.

From the shores of what used to be the New World, America's astronauts are now looking upward at still newer worlds to conquer. Of this new breed of explorers the first advance scouts have already set foot on the moon. It will not be long before other adventurers make landfall on Mars. After that, there are the other planets, other solar systems, the whole limitless reach of the universe to explore.

The techniques, skills, complex equipment, and sheer human bravery required for space travel make Columbus' crossing of the Atlantic seem simple. But, for all its fantastic differences, space exploration begins—just as did Columbus' voyage—with the setting-sail from an earthly harbor. And one of the hazards outside that harbor, a hazard that even a space ship must take into account, is the killer storm.

The "port of departure" for American space ships is Cape Kennedy, Florida, well inside hurricane territory. In the fall of 1964, when the Gemini space vehicle was about to be launched on its first unmanned test flight, a hurricane passed so near Cape Kennedy that the vehicle's Titan rocket had to be lowered from the gantry before the wind could blow it over—with the result that the Gemini was not tested until the spring of 1965. On several other occasions, the presence or likelihood of a hurricane in the vicinity has caused postponement of a vehicle's launching, because the storm threatened either the liftoff or the vehicle's recovery after splashdown.

# 3
# THE LAST OF
# LAST ISLAND

They were dancing on Last Island when the hurricane came.

There was always dancing on Last Island. In the years before the Civil War, this long, low, narrow arc of land off the Louisiana coast was the most fashionable, luxurious, and popular vacation resort in the South. It got its name—Last Island to the English-speaking population, Île Dernière to those who spoke French—because it was the westernmost and last in a necklace of islands that lay a few miles offshore in the Gulf of Mexico.

The Gulf edge of Last Island was a pearly white beach, twenty-five miles long. On the Caillou Bay side of the island, facing the Louisiana mainland, there was a sheltered inlet. Between the waters of the Gulf and the Bay, the island was a verdant slice of countryside.

Last Island had a permanent population of farmers and fisher-men, but they were usually outnumbered by vacationers. In August of 1856, the resort's four hundred guests represented a fair cross section of southern society—young and old, male and female, American and Creole French, rich and not so rich, of every calling from wealthy planter to riverboat gambler.

The island's hotel was one of the largest structures in Louisiana. Though it stood only two storeys high, it sprawled over a large area, and accommodated more people at one time than any hotel in the big city of New Orleans. The hotel backed on the inlet where the paddlewheel ferry *Star* docked, and had its own marina of landings and boathouses for private craft and yachts. The hotel's grounds consisted of acres of lawns, groves of oak trees bearded with Spanish moss, gardens of flowers, and a stretch of the island's beach. Dotted here and there about the grounds were the miniature cottages that many guests preferred, for their privacy, to the rooms and apartments in the main hotel building.

At each nightfall, the vacationers gathered in the hotel's ballroom. This room, too vast ever to be crowded, but always full, was truly the one most popular place on the whole island. The hotel's orchestra played for dancing. In the intervals between dances, the guests heard concerts and recitals by imported artists. It was said that, when the wind was right, even the muskrats and alligators of the mainland bayous crept out of their swampy dens to listen to the music that drifted over the Bay waters from Last Island.

Every night they danced on Last Island. Every night the dancing started right after dinner, and the first rays of the next day's rising sun found many of the guests still dancing. They were dancing on Last Island when the hurricane came.

This particular storm gave plenty of warning of its approach. The vacationers could have escaped it entirely, if only they had heeded its advance signals.

One day in early August, as tranquil as all the other summer days had been, the bathers on the Gulf-side beach of Last Island noticed an odd thing. Far out, where the horizon line of the ocean met the cloudless sky, the sea appeared to hump itself in a bulge. The raised mound of water darkened and lengthened, then surged forward toward the beach. The bathers retreated from the waterline and scampered to safety farther up the slope of the shore.

They felt a trifle foolish when the wave did arrive. It had looked like a towering cliff of water on the horizon, but it was less than two feet high when it got to the beach. Not even big enough to curl over when it broke, the wave spent itself in a sheet of quietly seething froth that did no more than swirl about the people's ankles.

Another wave came—just like the first—looking ugly as it swooped in from the Gulf, then subsiding playfully into froth as it reached the sand. And another came, and another; four of them altogether, and then no more. The whole sea quietened. The people calmed down, too, laughing at their brief panic as they relaxed on their beach chairs and blankets. And then, a few minutes later, the strangely heaving waves began anew—seven of them this time, one after another, and then again a lull.

"But what can be causing it?" asked someone. "There's not a breath of wind."

"And not a cloud in the sky," said another.

"No, but there must be a big blow going on somewhere out in the Gulf," said someone else.

He was right. A tremendous hurricane, born in the Caribbean Sea a week earlier, had moved northward past Cuba into the Gulf of Mexico, and now had temporarily ceased its forward progress. Its massive wheel of wind and cloud was still whirling furiously, but for the time being it was hesitating. Right now, the killer storm was roiling an empty patch of ocean four hundred miles south of Last Island. The storm's power can be gauged by the fact that the waves it raised could undulate across those four hundred miles of sea, and still be big enough to signal a warning to the people on that beach. However . . .

"Listen," said one of the ladies, gesturing back toward the hotel. "The music is beginning."

The sun was near setting; the hotel orchestra was tuning up; it was time for that night's dancing to commence, and the dancing was not to be missed. In minutes the beach was empty of people. Nothing remained but the oddly rhythmic waves that continued to wash up on the sands, a series of several in a row, with quiet pauses in between. Each new series of waves was just a little higher, a little heavier, a little stronger than the one before.

All night, while the revelers danced on Last Island, the sea grew more and more perturbed. And, although it could not yet be heard above the orchestra's playing, a wind had begun to blow from the northeast. At dawn, when a few of the dancers came outdoors to catch a breath of fresh air before retiring for a few hours' sleep, they found the air too gusty for comfort.

The waves were no longer arriving in that queer pulsating sequence of the day before. Now they were continuous, coming in at a sharp angle to the shore, and the wind had given each of them a fleecy whitecap. The bathing was brisk that day, what with the wind and the choppy surf, so not many swimmers stayed in the water for long. The beach was deserted by early afternoon, when a flock of scudding clouds began to obscure the sun.

None of the islanders could have known it, but the giant hurricane had begun to travel northward again—slowly, ponderously, but implacably—on a course that would hit the mainland of North America at the Louisiana coast. Between the hurricane and that coast lay the low, unprotected, shelterless Last Island, where still the people danced and made merry.

By the morning of August 9, the wind had become a steady gale from the northeast. The sky would have been completely overcast by cloud, except that the wind tore the clouds into rags and tatters, and between them the clear sky occasionally showed. The waves were immense and tumultuous now, coming in like ranks of great blue whales rolling sideways. They did not curl and break upon the sand like the combers of an ordinary high sea. Each time a wave reared up to crash upon the beach, the wind would catch it and rip away its crest in a spume of spray and foam. Although the sky overhead gleamed blue once in a while, and even sent down random shafts of sunlight, the island itself lay shrouded in a gray fog of swirling spindrift from the seashore.

Long afterward, the few people who lived through the Last Island hurricane remembered the peculiar sunset on that evening of August 9. The whole sky was covered now by the twisting, thrashing shreds of cloud, but near the western horizon the cloud veil tore apart for a few minutes, to give a glimpse of sky through which the sun slowly sank. It was a sky and a sun like none the people had ever seen before. The sky was a poison green, they said, and the sun the color of blood. After that brief and eerie sight, the clouds closed over the sky again and the night clamped down, black and noisy and wild.

The vacationers and even the long-time inhabitants of the island were beginning to get uneasy. "The wind grew weird," according to a contemporary description of the hurricane. "It ceased being a breath; it became a voice moaning across the world—hooting— uttering nightmare sounds."

Every kind of storm is noisy with the rush of wind. A hurricane wields such a continuous and mighty blast that its characteristic sound is a steady roar—so loud that even collapsing buildings seem to fall without a sound, their own crash inaudible in the general tumult. But the hurricane often comes with another sound, more awesome and even louder than its overall rumble. Other chroniclers of killer storms have mentioned noises as hair-raising as the nightmare sounds of the Last Island hurricane. Joseph Conrad, in his novel *Typhoon,* referred to "those wild and appalling shrieks that are heard at times passing mysteriously overhead in the steady roar of a hurricane," and he added that the "howls and shrieks seemed to take on something of human rage and pain. . . ."

Howling and moaning, hooting and shrieking, the wind beat about the Last Island hotel all night, a steady counterpoint to the music. There were other noises, too, the sounds of water rising and raging. The tempest of wind from the northeast was hurling the waters of Caillou Bay into the inlet that was the island's landing place. In the marina, the boats were grating against each other and jerking at their lines like terrified horses fighting their reins.

The next morning there seemed to be no air outside at all, but a solid atmosphere of wind-driven rain. It was not the clean, clear water that rain ought to be. It tasted of salt and it burned one's eyes and stung one's skin, because it was so mixed with spume torn from the sea waves and sand scooped up from the beach.

Some of the guests were becoming concerned about their situation now, and they ventured outside the hotel to look for reassurance. It was obvious that the frail sailboats in the marina could never put to sea in this weather. But so far, during the days the storm had been building up, the steamboat *Star* had managed to butt its way through the wind and waves each morning on its daily visit from the mainland. The people were anxious to see if the ferry could make the trip across Caillou Bay *this* morning. If the steamer arrived, well, the weather couldn't be quite as bad as it looked. And if the storm did get so violent that they'd have to flee the island, well, the *Star* would be there to carry them away.

Out in the Bay, the ferry's master was wondering if his little paddlewheel craft would survive the trip. The *Star* was already on its way to the island, though the waiting watchers could not see it yet through the rain and spindrift. Captain Abraham Smith had brought the steamer down the sheltered inland bayous without too much difficulty, but now it was out in the heaving waves of Caillou Bay with the northeast wind blowing from dead astern—and open water, with a following gale, is no place for a small craft to be.

(When a storm wind is directly behind a vessel, it blows the water forward as fast as the craft is moving, so neither the rudder nor the propeller has any "purchase" against the water, and the helmsman has almost no control of the ship's speed and direction. The only safe thing to do is to turn the craft's bow around to face into the wind and the windblown waves. With the seas washing *toward* the ship, the rudder and propeller can again bite into the water and hold the ship sufficiently steady to ride out the blow. But in the case of the *Star,* if it was to reach Last Island, south of the mainland, it *had* to scud dangerously along with the northeast blast at its back.)

Somehow the *Star* got there, though afterward Captain Smith said he had no idea how he'd done it. Waiting on the hotel's verandas, the wind-buffeted and rain-drenched vacationers cheered. Then they ran indoors to spread the word that "the *Star* is here!" The tense and worried guests relaxed; rescue was at hand if it was needed. To keep the people in good cheer, the hotel manager ordered his orchestra to assemble, though it was still only early afternoon. The ballroom filled with music, then with dancers, as the guests gladly exchanged their earlier worries for one more round of merriment.

Outside in the *Star*'s pilothouse, Captain Smith heard with astonishment the scraps of music the wind blew to him. He couldn't understand why the people should be celebrating. The captain realized what the islanders had not: that the *Star* would be no use to them as a means of escape. The Bay waters had been blown into the inlet until they overflowed its banks. The ferryboat was now anchored in its accustomed landing spot, but there was no longer a patch of ground anywhere to lay a gangplank on. The flood waters were not deep enough for the vessel to maneuver closer to dry land, but they were too deep and turbulent for a human being to cross. The captain and crew couldn't get off the ship, and the islanders couldn't get on.

For the moment, the people on shore—being indoors and dry, at least, and ignorant of their peril—were in a better situation than those on the steamboat. Captain Smith and his men were out on deck in the teeth of the storm, fighting to save their vessel. Even after they had thrown out three heavy anchors, the steamer was still being blown and shoved around the inlet.

The afternoon had become as dark, noisy, and violent as the

inside of a concrete-mixing machine. The wind was like a driving piston, slamming before it such a volume of water—mingled rain and spray—that it was impossible to see where the ocean left off and the air began. Every few seconds, the darkness was riven and utterly abolished by a writhing, jagging, forking flash of lightning. But the thunder that usually accompanies lightning could not be noticed—the rolling cannonade of the hurricane's own noise was too overwhelmingly loud.

A gentleman in the hotel's ballroom decided to sit out the next dance, and retired to the sidelines to light a cigar. Something hissed behind him and his match blew out. The man turned and discovered a tiny aperture in the mahogany-panelled wall. It was no bigger than a nail hole, but through it the hurricane wind was hissing with the noise and force of a broken steam pipe.

A steward, circulating through the ballroom with a tray of drinks, paused to look out a window. Beyond the reflection of the gliding dancers, there was nothing to be seen but the rain streaming down the glass. Down? No, it was pouring *up* the windowpane. The steward was mildly puzzled; he'd never known rain to behave that way before. Had he been outdoors on the windward side of the hotel, he would have seen that the rain wasn't falling; it was being blasted along parallel to the ground like a wind-borne river. When it hit the building, it streamed *up* the hotel's two-storey front and smoked off its rooftop like the spindrift from the ocean's storm-torn waves.

In outlying areas of the island, the more exposed cottages and farmhouses began to rock ominously. Here a brick chimney tumbled. There a window shutter wrenched itself free and disappeared on the wind. Elsewhere a front porch came loose from its house, came apart, and sailed away in pieces. One cottage's entire roof lifted tentatively, settled back for a moment, then peeled off the house like the lid off a sardine tin, and flapped away into the darkness. Another house tilted slowly, as if pushed by a giant's gentle but determined hand. It slid off its stone foundation, paused for a time, then continued moving, grating across what had been its kitchen garden, shedding doors and boards and things until it disintegrated into rubble.

None of these events made a sound that could be heard.

As the island's smaller houses began to fall, their panicky occupants groped their way toward the big hotel. It was built of stout timbers; it would stand. Many of the people toiling through the storm never reached the hotel. The air was full of deadly flying objects. Pieces of houses, torn-off branches, uprooted trees careened like dark meteors across the island. Unseen, unheard, impossible to dodge, they struck and killed and kept on going.

The *Star,* its anchors helpless to hold it against the storm, was still pitching and wallowing and grinding against the island banks. Captain Smith decided that the ship's only salvation lay in lessening the surface it presented to the wind. He gave the order to cut away all of the steamer's upper works, and his crew set to with axes and crowbars. Overboard went the two tall smokestacks, the pilothouse, the deck cabins.

Now little more than a hull, the *Star* was not quite so battered by the wind, and, being lighter, floated somewhat higher in the water. Captain Smith found that he could now maneuver the steamer to within a few dozen yards of the hotel's rear veranda. He was close enough to see that every window was festively aglow with candlelight, and to hear the orchestra still playing lustily.

"Dancing!" snorted the captain. "If this wind shifts around to the south, there'll be a dance of another kind!"

Captain Smith was aware that, for a hurricane, this was a fairly mild one—so far. But he couldn't tell which way it was traveling. Right now, the hurricane's eye was still somewhere south of Last Island. Of the great ring of wind which spun around that center, Last Island was receiving the segment that blew from the north. This was a blessing, because the hurricane was shoving with it from the south a stupendous swell of Gulf water. So long as the wind continued from the north it was holding back the advance of that great wave. But, if the storm should pass Last Island in such a way that the other rim of its circle of wind raked the island, that wind would be blowing from the south. Instead of holding back the hurricane wave, the south wind would give it an added impetus. The waters would heap up to mountainous heights, and they would be hurled upon the low-lying island like an avalanche.

"It would knock Last Island clear to Canada," the captain muttered grimly.

And just as he said it, the wind—which had been blowing now for several days on end—suddenly slackened and stopped. The ferryboat, so long tilted sideways by the blast, rocked abruptly upright and nearly pitched the captain off his feet. The unexpected silence, after the storm's sustained roar, made every crewman feel that he had gone stone deaf on the instant.

The dancers inside the hotel realized that they could hear themselves talking without shouting, and the orchestra's music rang out louder. A number of people stepped outside to see what the weather looked like. They found that the rain had stopped with the wind, and the clouds overhead seemed thinner. But still the day felt uncomfortably odd. The atmosphere was an unearthly copper color, hot and unpleasant to breathe. The outdoors seemed so strange and unfriendly that the people hurried back into the security of the hotel. They didn't notice that the *Star*'s bell was ringing frantically to attract their attention.

It is hard to believe that not one of the people on Last Island was familiar with the workings of a hurricane. But evidently only Captain Smith knew the meaning of this lull in the storm. The hurricane's eye, its calm center, was passing directly over Last Island. How long the calm might last, the captain couldn't guess, but he knew very well what would come after it. Right *now* was the one and only and last opportunity to load the islanders aboard his boat and get them safely away.

He never did. The crewmen threw out grappling hooks with ropes attached, hoping to haul the steamer, hand over hand, as close as possible to the hotel's rear veranda. But the calm was over too soon—this hurricane's eye was a small one. The wind came again, like a bludgeon, bringing with it more rain and, in between the blazes of lightning, the darkness of deepest night.

It came from the south. It blew from the other shore of Last Island, across the beach and past the Gulf face of the hotel. The *Star* recoiled from the blow, snapping the ropes that had just been secured, and began to slide away from the hotel's veranda. Captain Smith watched in anguish as the brightly lighted ballroom windows dwindled and dimmed with distance.

But still they danced on Last Island. With the people's retreat into the hotel again, after their one brief look at the forbidding outdoors, they seem to have decided to pretend that the storm did not exist. It must have been a difficult pretense, for they had living proof of the hurricane's horror right there indoors with them. The hotel was now more crowded than ever, with the native islanders who had fled from their homes to its shelter. They were drying their sodden clothes before the fireplaces, having their wounds and bruises treated, and lamenting the destruction of a home or the disappearance of a loved one.

But the vacationers seemed determined to disbelieve in reality. They returned to their dancing—while outside, all along the island, stands of sugarcane and live oak trees were falling before the storm. The farmhouses and barns and cottages that had been weakened by the hurricane's first broadside were now collapsing under the second. Down on the beach—but there was no beach to be seen—the Gulf waters, unleashed by the change of wind, had climbed the sandy slope and covered it, and now each new wave was pushing farther up the hotel's lawns.

On the other side of Last Island, the *Star* had finally been marooned, atop one of the flood-covered banks of what used to be the mouth of the inlet. It was still battered by the wind there, grinding and crunching against the rocks that held it, but the rugged little steamer showed no signs yet of coming to pieces. Captain Smith and his men tied ropes about their waists and made them fast to the ship's railings.

In the hotel's ballroom, one girl gave a little squeak of dismay and stepped back from her dancing partner to look down at her feet; her silken slippers were wet; rivulets of black water were spreading and staining the polished floor. The streams were edging in from under the front veranda doors. Rapidly they merged into a single sheet that covered the dance floor and eddied around the feet of the crowd. Some of the women began to whimper with fright, while the men helped them to perch on chairs and stools. Bellboys brought lanterns and shone them out the front windows. As far as the beams could reach, there was nothing *but* water.

Then, out of the Gulf, out of the darkness, out-roaring the hurricane itself, rumbled a noise that was more felt than heard, as if it vibrated the very bones inside one's flesh. The hotel shook. The crystal chandeliers swung and jangled wildly, plaster flaked down from the ceilings, dishes clattered off tables, people staggered and fell. But it was not just the building shaking now. It was the ground under it, the whole island, trembling under the impact of a moving mountain of water, the hurricane wave. It hit Last Island with the shock of an earthquake, and thundered right over it—and almost everything that stood or grew or lived on Last Island was obliterated, instantly and forever.

At the hotel, the ballroom's tall windows were the first things to go. They exploded inward and through each one burst a cataract of water that caught up the windows' splinters and churned with broken glass. For a few seconds, the big room was a whirlpool full of careening furniture and tumbling bodies. The water frothed pink with a mixture of foam and blood, and a babble of screams and prayers mingled with the uproar of destruction.

But that bedlam of seething, slashing carnage lasted only a few seconds—for everything was happening now much faster than can be told. The front wall of the hotel buckled immediately after the windows. It caved into the ballroom with most of the hotel's veranda crashing in behind it, and with still more tons of water behind that. The room was now a welter of tables and chairs, drowning people, porch steps and banisters, bleeding people, thrashing draperies and tapestries, crushed people, violins and flutes, and still-cascading ocean. With the front wall gone, there was nothing to hold up that end of the ceiling's massive oaken beams, and they smashed down one after another into the melée below. The beams had supported the hotel's second storey, so that too crumbled, spilling into the ballroom all the upstairs rooms full of beds, lamps, wardrobes, people who had gone to bed. . . .

However, almost simultaneous with all this, the monster wave had jolted the hotel entirely off its foundations. As the whole building reared backward and broke apart, the ballroom ceased to be a room. It, like every other room in the hotel, simply dissolved into separate walls, then separate boards, then indistinguishable fragments that all went swirling and whirling away on the wave, in company with billiard tables, stable horses, kitchen stoves, candlesticks, dancing shoes. . . . Everything was washed into the marina to join the wreckage of the boats there, then out through the inlet to scatter or sink at last in Caillou Bay.

Meanwhile, as the sea waters continued to smash across Last Island, they literally tore the island in two. They chewed through a wide swath of the beach, then scoured away the higher land where the hotel had stood, then sluiced all that land down the other side of the island and dumped it into Caillou Bay. The sea had carved for itself a new channel a mile wide, right through the entire island from the Gulf to the Bay.

By the time the sea waves had plowed their way through the island, they had spent some of their original terrible momentum. The main torrent billowed into the Bay with not quite enough force to swamp the ferryboat *Star*. As that mass of water rushed by it, the steamer bobbed up like a cork from the rocks on which it was grounded. Then it stayed afloat and miraculously stayed upright.

By the intermittent flash of the lightning, Captain Smith could see the pieces of ruins and flotsam that tumbled through the waters around his craft, and he could see that they included an occasional human form. Bravely, the captain and his crewmen dove overboard to rescue anyone they could. They had only the rope lifelines to keep themselves from drowning or being washed helplessly out into the Bay. Yet they plunged repeatedly into the maw of black water that gnashed at them with sharp and heavy chunks of wreckage. They hauled aboard one body after another, and their efforts were rewarded when they discovered that an occasional one of the victims was still alive.

There had been four hundred visitors vacationing on Last Island in that August of 1856. No one had ever bothered to count how many other people were workers in the hotel, and no census had ever been taken of the farming and fishing families who lived permanently on the island. So it will never be known how many people died in the hurricane that destroyed Last Island. Of the victims that Captain Smith and his men dredged from the water, fewer than forty lived.

Days later, when the killer storm had swept on inland past the Louisiana coast, other rescue boats hurried out to Last Island. They found the *Star,* again grounded high and dry when the storm waters subsided, and they took off her crew and living passengers. Then the rescuers searched the ravaged island. They found not a single building or tree still standing and they found only one other living creature: a cow, trying to make a meal of the salt-encrusted grass in what had been her home meadow. How that one animal survived the shambles is still a mystery. The rescue vessels sailed home again, and left Last Island to its desolation.

If you look for Last Island on a map now, you'll find it marked as Last Islands or Îles Dernières—plural—because it ceased being one island when the hurricane of 1856 tore it in half. Since then other storms have hacked other channels across it, and today it is a chain of islets separated by gaps of water.

As the years passed, the drifting sands filled the crumbled foundations of the vanished buildings, and sifted between the bleached ribs of what was once the plucky steamboat *Star*. None but an occasional gray pelican came to visit the island afterward, and nothing grew there again but stunted scrub trees, wild prairie-cane, and the sparse dune grasses that wave in the sea wind, there on Last Island, where once the people danced.

# 4
# A KILLER IS BORN

We have just watched a hurricane as it was seen by its victims on Last Island. That is, our view was from ground level. Through all the eons that man has lived on earth, until just a generation ago, that was the *only* way he ever saw a hurricane—from the victim's viewpoint, underneath it.

It was less than thirty years ago that an airplane pilot dared to fly for the first time into the upper levels of a hurricane and see it from the bird's-eye view. It was not until the 1950's that man was able to see the killer storm from a safe distance, its shape "drawn" for him on a cathode screen by the electronic blips of radar. And it was not until the 1960's that man first looked directly down on a hurricane from high enough to see it in its entirety, when satellites carrying cameras first photographed the storms from orbits in outer space.

As long as man could see the hurricane only from underneath, and only an extremely small part of it at any one time, he could do no more than guess at its overall shape. As recently as thirty years ago, it was thought that the hurricane was shaped like a doughnut

—a circular roll of storm clouds surrounding the eye, a clear-cut hole of calmer air. Since then, high-altitude photographs have shown us that the hurricane is really a more lopsided and ragged shape, rather like a child's pinwheel—a tremendous spiral instead of a circle. From the hurricane's eye (where the pinwheel's pin would be), thick coils of cloud unwind until they're strung out in long trailing streamers (like the pinwheel's vanes).

Though we speak today of "killer" storms, it is likely that there could have been no life whatever on this planet without them. In the primordial time of Earth's beginning, some three or four billion years ago, after it had cooled from a blob into a solid globe, its entire atmosphere was one all-encompassing envelope of raging, boiling storm that thundered around and over the rocky surface of the whole world. In a manner that is still unknown, the unending storm's incessant bolts of high-tension lightning gradually worked a change in a few of the elements that made up the atmosphere. From being lifeless chemicals, they were somehow energized by the lightning's electricity into complex organic compounds that had a dim vitality of their own.

These sparks of life drifted down from the storm cover into the planet's warm waters. In that "nutrient broth" the newly created compounds continued to develop in complexity, and to link together with other chemicals. In the course of time—many more millions of years—they eventually gave rise to specks of protoplasm, primitive but definitely living organisms, capable of reproducing and multiplying and developing still further. Out of that storm-born start of life arose every living thing—from mosses to mankind—that inhabits the world today.

Back at the beginning of time the killer storms weren't killers, but creators, and they had a reason for being. Even nowadays—though it may seem to accomplish no more than mass ruination and mass murder—the most destructive hurricane can have its good points and, as we shall see in later chapters, directly or indirectly bring benefits that may excuse some of the harm it does. Even if the hurricane were an unmitigated evil, there is (to date) no means of doing away with it entirely, except by "turning off" the sun, an alternative which is both impossible and unthinkable. Just as the sun is responsible for keeping the earth alive, so is it responsible for causing all of the earth's weather, including hurricanes, typhoons, tornadoes, and every lesser storm.

If there were no sun to affect it, the earth's covering of air would lie perfectly still and windless. However, when the sun warms an area of air, its heat makes the air's gas molecules begin to vibrate briskly. The molecules bump and shove each other farther apart, so their particular area of air expands and becomes lighter in weight. This lighter air tends to rise, and the cooler, heavier air around slides under the warm air into the space it is vacating. The movements of these areas of air are felt as wind.

If the earth were a smooth ball of one material, sunshine and wind would be the only "weather" it would have, and that wind would perpetually follow the same paths around the planet. But the earth isn't smooth. It's wrinkled and bumpy with mountains and gullies; these deflect and disarrange the wind's patterns. And the earth is surfaced with a variety of materials: bare soil, rocks, desert sands, fields of grass, forests of trees, freshwater ponds, saltwater oceans, concrete cities. Each of these reflects or absorbs the sun's rays in varying degrees, and so complicates the heating or cooling of the air in its vicinity.

Most important, nearly three quarters of the globe is surfaced with water. The sun's effect on that is much the same as it is on the air. Its heat causes the water's component molecules to vibrate and jostle each other apart. Those molecules bumped upward from the water's surface continue to rise in the columns of warm air which are ascending at the same time. This process is known as evaporation, and it happens wherever there is moisture.

The evaporated water molecules are borne upward until they reach a height where the air is cooler. There they slow their vibrations and condense—clump together in groups—forming tiny water droplets, and a visible cloud appears. The cloud sails along with the prevailing wind until it reaches an even cooler area or en-counters floating dust particles, and another change takes place. The droplets cluster even closer together and begin to merge into larger drops.

The droplets would never merge without some solid central core or "nucleus" around which to gather. Sometimes they provide this themselves; when a cloud of water vapor moves into very cold air, groups of the droplets freeze into tiny ice crystals, and become the nuclei for other droplets to condense around and form snowflakes. More often, though, it is drifting dust particles—ever present in the air—which become the cores for droplets to gather around and make larger, heavier drops.

Either way, the water vapor becomes heavy enough to plummet from the cloud. It may fall directly as raindrops or it may fall as snowflakes. But these too (except in winter) melt into raindrops as they descend through warmer air. And so, finally, the water evaporated from the earth's surface—perhaps months before—re-turns to the earth as rain.

Those three components—sunshine and the wind and rain which it causes—give the world its varied climates and weathers. (Climate refers to the general conditions in a large area, such as the wet and dry seasons of the tropics. Weather means the daily changing conditions in a more localized area.) Both climate and weather are affected by a multitude of other factors: the earth's gravity, rotation and magnetism; the movement of ocean currents; the different altitudes and composition of land masses; volcanic eruptions; meteor showers; sunspots; and even city smog and the vapor contrails of high-flying aircraft. But sunshine, wind, and rain are the basic ingredients. Whether they interact to cause a gentle shower, a warm breeze, or a cataclysmic hurricane, they are merely obeying natural physical laws.

One of these laws is that energy can in no way be destroyed; it exists forever, merely changing from one form to another. Heat and light are two forms of energy, and they are constantly being beamed at the earth by the sun. It is difficult to express in words or figures the awesome amount of energy the sun manufactures or to tell what it means in terms of usable power, except to say that it runs the earth and everything on it.

The solar energy that arrives in the form of light is utilized by plants. They change the light energy into chemical energy that makes them grow, bloom, and fruit. That energy is passed along to the animals that eat the plants, who utilize the chemical energy to keep them alive and power their movements. Much of the solar energy that arrives on earth in the form of heat stirs the air into wind currents and the water into air-borne vapor. When the heated vapor cools and condenses into drops, it exchanges its heat energy for mechanical energy, that is, the weight of the drops and the force they exert when they fall.

Because the evaporation of water is an invisible and fairly slow process, we may not realize just what a weight of water the sun is sucking into the sky every minute, and how much energy that involves. But a single summer cloud, a mile wide, a mile long, and a mile tall may contain a quantity of water weighing as much as a battleship. If the whole cloud were to condense and fall as rain, it would release into the sky some four quadrillions of calories of heat (enough to melt a sizable iceberg) and the cloud's water would shower onto the earth with a total force of 70,000 tons.

The mechanical energy expended in that rain's splashing onto a mountaintop may not do any useful work. But as the water collects into a stream and continues running downhill, its mechanical energy can be harnessed by a waterwheel and utilized to turn a primitive mill. Or the running water can spin a hydroelectric dam's generator that changes the mechanical energy into electrical energy and so provides power and light for a whole county.

Quite often, wind and water vapor convert their stored-up solar energy directly into electrical energy without any help from man's machinery. In a storm, the fierce currents of wind batter the water droplets about in such a way that—colliding, being mashed together, being torn apart—they build up charges of static electricity. Each drop's charge is insignificant, but all together they total a tremendous electrical potential. When this charge accumulates to the point where it *has* to discharge, within the clouds or between the clouds and the earth, we see a lightning bolt. In the instant of tearing through the air, the discharge exchanges part of its electrical energy for both light energy and heat energy. The light is the visible flash. The heat is imparted to the surrounding air so suddenly that the air expands in a minor explosion, or thunder.

At every moment, the air is a mighty powerhouse full of energy stored in its winds and the water vapor they carry. At every moment, the sunlight streaming through the atmosphere is pumping into it still more energy. That energy cannot be destroyed, but must be used, moved, put to work, changed into other forms. And it can change gradually or violently.

For one example of the violent, some of the atmosphere's energy is let loose in the "jet streams," currents of wind that roar around the world at more than 300 miles per hour—but so many miles above the earth that they don't directly or immediately affect the surface. The weather generally dispenses its energy in milder ways and smaller doses—tolerable winds, ordinary rains, unremarkable snowfalls—because there are numerous balancing factors which hold it under control. For one thing, the planet is big enough that when tremendous forces build up in one area of the atmosphere there is usually a more quiescent area elsewhere for the forces to expand into without any noticeable disturbance.

But sometimes, even in placid areas of the atmosphere, the elements of sunshine, air, and water combine in such a way that they overcome or evade the various forces that hold the weather within moderate bounds. When that happens, the expenditure of energy becomes almost as violent as that in the jet streams, and it is expended at a lower level where we can feel it and suffer from it. Depending on the season of the year and the local conditions, it may take the form of a drenching cloudburst, an extraordinary thunderstorm, a blizzard, a windstorm, a tornado, a hurricane.

Of the many ways that weather can run wild, the hurricane is an outstanding example, because it *always* starts in a calm and tranquil area of the atmosphere. On a hot day in the late summer of the year, somewhere in the Atlantic Ocean a few hundred miles north of the equator, the sun shines down from a cloudless sky onto an open, empty part of the sea that's almost as still as a pond. The water heaves gently, but there are no discernible waves, and the breeze is too mild even to ruffle the sea's surface. There is activity going on, nevertheless.

As always, the sun is evaporating water from the ocean's surface, and that invisible vapor is being carried skyward by the rising currents of sun-warmed air. Something like thirty gallons of water are being lifted every minute from every acre of the sea. When the warm, moisture-laden air rises from this section of the ocean it cannot leave a vacuum behind; as it departs, other air is sucked into its place. This is cooler, heavier air which started its journey from miles and miles away, from a place where perhaps the sun was screened by clouds.

The cooler air comes as a wind, of course, but it does not simply slide straight into this new location. (As a matter of fact, no wind that blows on earth moves in a perfectly straight line.) Cool air is dense air, its molecules packed closely together. Weathermen refer to a mass of cool, dense air as a high pressure area, or just "a High," and you might think of it as air heaped into a mound. As the air flows down from that mound, the earth's rotation gives it a gentle twist to the right, so that it swoops in a clockwise spiral rather than a straight line. It twines down from the High as if it were following a gently descending road down and around a mountainside. Then, as this wind reaches a low pressure area (a Low) of warmer, less densely packed air, it reverses its curve. The wind continues its downward flow, as if it were following a gently descending road

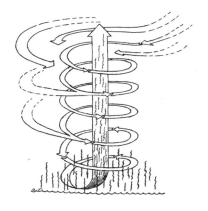

*As the cool winds spiral and settle into an area vacated by the uprising "chimney" of warm air, they themselves are warmed and ascend, thus bringing in still more cool air from afar.*

down and around the inside of a valley bowl, but now it turns in a leftward-bending or *counter*clockwise spiral.*

In that empty, open stretch of the Atlantic Ocean, the sun has warmed a great mass of air, lightened its density, and created an immense low pressure area over the sea. Cooler air is drawn into this Low from a High many miles away, and it arrives here like an airplane circling to land, settling down toward sea level in ever-tightening counterclockwise circles.

While it is swooping, spiraling, and settling, however, this air is also being warmed by the sun overhead. The new air has scarcely arrived before it has also become warm and light enough to follow the earlier air aloft. So the cycle continues: warm air rising, being replaced by cooler air, which in turn gets warm and ascends, thus dragging in a still newer supply of air from afar.

Meanwhile, the fresh air, arriving as it does in a tightening spiral, forms a "chimney" effect around the warm air that is continuously rising from the ocean surface. This chimney constricts the warm

* Only in the northern hemisphere does the air move as described—clockwise down from a High and counterclockwise into a Low. South of the equator it behaves just the opposite: sliding down counterclockwise from a High and clockwise into a Low.

air's upward passage, so it has to rise even faster than before. This drags the cool air in faster, too, so its spiral tightens, constricting the chimney still more, and the warm air has to go up it even more rapidly. The entire system of circulation moves faster and faster— cool air whipping around and down and into the system, warm air swooshing upward.

This sounds like quite a windstorm already, but actually it takes place over such a tremendous area of ocean and involves such great volumes of air that its movement might seem no more than a stiff breeze to a sailor on the sea. Despite the titanic amounts of energy involved, this atmospheric disturbance is still a fairly fragile thing. An adverse wind butting in from another direction could disarrange its whirling pattern.

However, even in its first few hours of life, this budding storm has packed away a store of reserve energy. Remember all the water —thirty gallons per acre per minute—that has been borne aloft all this time, in the form of water vapor carried by the rising air currents. Millions of gallons have been lifted by now, every single molecule carrying its store of heat energy.

Eventually the uprushing column of moisture-laden air reaches a high, cold altitude where it begins to cool and slow down. The molecules crowd together and, as the coolness slows their heat-vibrations, they begin to merge and condense into droplets, letting go some of their heat energy as they do so. The heat which they release warms *this* level of atmosphere, so that the next puff of up-draft coming along behind them goes a little higher before *it* begins to slow and cool. There, of course, the updraft's moisture again condenses, again releases its heat content, and again warms the surrounding atmosphere. In effect, this process keeps extending the chimney higher and higher, providing more altitude for the central updraft to climb through, and thus to suck in more of that spiraling indraft at the chimney's bottom, near sea level.

At the same time, the chimney itself, which so far has been just an invisible effect of circulating winds, now becomes real and visible. The vapors condensed into droplets have become clouds, great banks of them wheeling around the chimney. The centrifugal force of their revolution holds them outward a distance of some miles from the storm's central axis point, so there is an open vertical area up through the clouds' center. Since that central area remains too warm for any vapor to condense there, it stays free of clouds as long as the storm lasts. It is now, quite visibly, the "eye" of the storm.

The bulk of the cloud wheel extends into the cooler air around the storm, and in that cooler air the clouds' droplets condense still further, into ice crystals which, falling from the clouds, melt into

*At the very top of this cutaway sketch of a full-grown hurricane is the pale "veil" of ice-crystal cloud with its fringe of "rooster tails." Beneath it is the hurricane proper, its eye surrounded by great whirling walls and vaults of spiral clouds, from which rain pelts down onto the ocean below. The sea inside the eye merely tosses in confusion, but under the wheel of clouds it races along with the winds. The scraps of dark cloud in the foreground are the low-flying, outflung "scud." This drawing is exaggerated in scale to show the storm's details. Actually, since a hurricane stands about 8 miles high and may be 250 miles in diameter, its shape is more like that of a phonograph record, with the eye for its "spindle hole."*

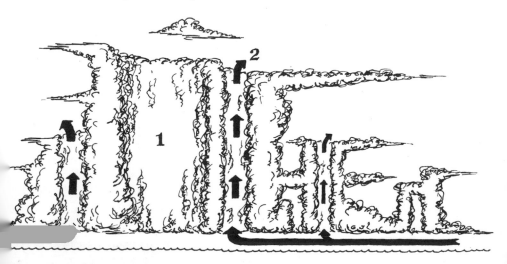

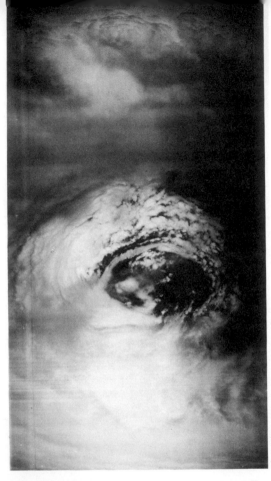

*The central chimney or eye of a hurricane.*

ESSA

rain. The storm has already gorged itself with so much moisture that its rain, when it finally falls, is a veritable deluge. Even so, it takes a considerable while to reach the sea beneath, because the circling winds seize it and drive it before them through the sky.

For what started as a weather "disturbance"—just three or four days ago—has by this time become a full-fledged hurricane. It towers some eight miles into the sky. Its great turning wheel of cloud and rain is anywhere from 50 to 250 miles in diameter. Its central chimney, or eye, may be 5 to 20 miles across. (The eye of a hurricane that passed over Jacksonville, Florida, in 1944 was 70 miles in diameter.) Up and through the cloud walls around that eye pour perhaps a million tons of warm air per second. To feed that updraft, the chimney gulps in at its lower end so much fresh air from the outside that the counterclockwise-spiraling winds are now moving at speeds of more than 75 miles an hour as they near the eye, and may attain 150 to 200 miles per hour as the hurricane continues to grow. Even at the farthest edges of the cloud wheel, perhaps a hundred miles from the eye, the winds hurrying toward the hurricane's chimney may be moving at gale force speeds of 40 to 50 miles an hour. The hundreds or thousands of square miles of ocean beneath the storm have become just as tormented as the air around it—heaving, tossing, raging.

Obviously the storm is no longer a fragile thing that could be dispersed by a change in the weather conditions outside itself. It has become a self-contained, self-operating, self-perpetrating energy engine. The fresh air it devours from hundreds of miles around is its "fuel." The engine gulps it, warms it inside its hot chimney, rushes it upward, extracts its moisture to make more clouds and rain, extracts its heat to keep the chimney hot, and spews out the used air as "exhaust" at the top of its chimney.

This atmospheric engine's energy turnover is almost unbelievable. To illustrate it in different ways:

The hurricane's energy expenditure in *one day,* if converted into electric current, would be sufficient to run all the electrical equipment in the United States—from kitchen toasters to the factories of General Motors—for more than *six months.*

Or: in *one day* the hurricane unleashes energy equivalent to what would be expended in *eighty earthquakes* of the magnitude that demolished San Francisco in 1906.

Or: in *one day* the heat energy released by a hurricane is equal to the heat that would blast from the simultaneous explosion of *four hundred hydrogen bombs* of 20-megaton size.

That's in one day. On the average, a hurricane's active life lasts anywhere from eight to twelve days. Some have lived for a month. During that time, so long as it is over open sea where it can keep on devouring heat and moisture, the hurricane goes on getting bigger and stronger.

The relationship between a hurricane's strength and its sources of energy is so evident that sometimes weathermen can guess, simply from the wallop it packs, where the storm originated. The hurricanes that do the worst damage in the United States seem to be those born the farthest *away* from America—in the area of the Cape Verde Islands, 300 miles off the coast of Africa. Starting from there, they have an open stretch of 2,500 miles of warm tropical ocean to cross, picking up and packing in energy all the way, before slamming like a sledge-hammer into the West Indies or the American mainland. One of the most damaging hurricanes ever to hit the New England states, the great storm of 1938, came from even farther away. It got its start as an area of low pressure over the hot sands of the Sahara desert. As the Low moved westward out of Africa onto the ocean, it quickly took on the typical hurrican configuration.

Typhoons in the Pacific Ocean can be bigger and more violent than the Atlantic's fiercest hurricanes, simply because the Pacific is wider. The typhoons have more warm water available for their initial energy build-up, and more room to grow in, before they reach and devastate some land mass. An Atlantic hurricane is regarded as "one of the big ones" if its central winds hit a hundred and fifty miles per hour. A Pacific typhoon the same number of days old may pack winds blowing at *two* hundred and fifty miles an hour.

It has been calculated that a hurricane or typhoon cannot be formed anywhere except above a body of water that has been warmed to at least 82° Fahrenheit. This would account for one curiosity about these killer storms: they occur over every tropical sea on earth *except* the Atlantic Ocean south of the equator. This is the Atlantic's deepest and widest part, extending into both the Indian and Antarctic oceans, and evidently there is too much cold water there for the sun ever to warm enough of it to the necessary temperature.

This has been an extremely simplified description of a killer storm's birth and growth to maturity. But, in its essentials, it is all that the weathermen *know* about the storm's development, and they frankly admit that they don't know enough. For instance, the foregoing description leaves a lot of questions unanswered. One of the most important is: why aren't there *more* such storms than there are?

The conditions cited as being necessary for the birth of the storm—a cloudless, nearly windless sky; the sun beating down; a calm ocean warmed to at least 82°F.—these conditions exist almost all the time somewhere in the tropic waters of the Atlantic just north of the equator. If they were all that were required, hurricanes should be continuously forming in those parts, and churning off on their journeys of destruction, one right behind another like an endless freight train of cars loaded with dynamite.

But not more than an average of five hurricanes grow to full maturity in that area each year. So there must be some additional weather condition necessary to their birth, some "secret ingredient" that has not been discovered yet.

The weathermen have various theories as to what that necessary "extra" might be. Some believe that the earth's rotation is not enough to account for the wind's initial twist that starts it spiraling downward and inward around the baby storm's center. They think the wind may begin to veer in a circle because the storm is born on the border between two air masses of different temperatures and densities. A wind blowing between the two masses would move faster on the warmer, less dense side, and this would start it curving inward toward the other side. Other weathermen believe that the storm gets its first twirl when a moving wall of wind collides with a block of absolutely calm air. At the point where the two masses "sideswipe," a slice of the calm air would be peeled off and set to spinning.

Either of these conditions—two air masses of different composition side by side, or a moving air mass colliding with a stationary one—would be infrequent enough to account for the comparative "rarity" of hurricanes. The trouble is that such conditions are *too* infrequent. There is no evidence that they ever occur at all in the Atlantic regions where hurricanes are born.

A more plausible theory is that the hurricane's chimney-and-updraft effect depends on some freakish weather condition. The experts who hold this opinion refuse to believe that the storm, all by itself, could pump out enough "exhaust" air from the top of its chimney to allow the continued gulping-in of new "fuel" air at the bottom. They think that the hurricane's chimney, working on its own, would fill up with air faster than it could spew it upward, and so its whole system would clog to a standstill. If this supposition is correct, there would have to be an extra pump working some-

*Hurricane Beulah, in the Gulf of Mexico off the coast of Texas, seen from satellite ESSA-3, on September 19, 1967.*

*ESSA*

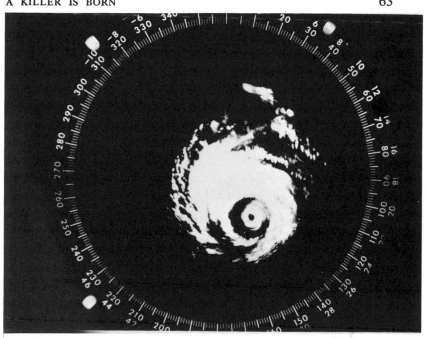

*Hurricane Beulah has now approached within range of the United States'
"radar fence," and you are watching its imminent arrival on a Brownsville,
Texas, weather bureau radarscope.*

ESSA

where up above the storm. The theorists believe that there would
have to exist either a low pressure pocket in the upper atmosphere,
to suck up the excess rising air, or a high-altitude wind moving
across the top of the chimney, to blow it away.

Whether any of these theories about the hurricane's "secret
ingredient" is correct or not, no one can prove or disprove. For one
reason, we never know when or where a hurricane is being born
until it is fairly well along in its development. Even the orbiting
weather satellites cannot yet recognize a hurricane until it has
acquired its characteristic spiral pattern. By then the weather is so
chaotic that weathermen can't tell what might have been the original
conditions in the area, or decide which of them contributed to the
storm's beginning.

The most recent and most revolutionary suggestion as to what causes a hurricane is the idea of Dr. Joseph M. Prospero, a marine scientist, who was working on the Caribbean island of Barbados when he noticed that an occasional wind dusted the island with microscopic particles of sand identical to the sand of the Sahara desert in Africa, more than 3,000 miles from Barbados.

Dr. Prospero believes that sandstorms over the Sahara send their tinier particles blowing westward across the Atlantic. He suggests that these swarms of microscopic grains—acting as nuclei and collecting the water droplets in the clouds they encounter—start the droplets' condensation into larger drops, and thus the energy exchanges which start to build a hurricane. Dr. Prospero is presently conducting experiments to test his theory. If it turns out to be correct, then at least *some* of the killer storms really begin when a sandstorm blows up in the Sahara desert. (The qualifier "some" has to be added because, obviously, the Sahara-sandstorm theory would not account for other hurricane-type storms like the Pacific typhoon.)

Meanwhile, that specimen hurricane has grown in three or four days from an invisible combination of atmospheric conditions into a runaway energy engine. Anyone who saw this dark and rampaging giant now would not wonder so much about how it began; he'd worry more about how it might be stopped.

But even if we could somehow turn off the sun that built this engine, it has gathered into its far-sprawling system so much energy by now that it would churn on for as long as twelve more days before faltering for lack of fuel. Since the sun *does* still shine above it, beaming still more energy down into the atmosphere and ocean that support it, the storm's supply of available fuel is inexhaustible, and it is conceivable that the hurricane *could* rage on indefinitely. However, other factors do get involved in the situation. They eventually put a brake to the storm's mighty engine so that it slows and stops, though usually not before it has done a deal of damage—because the storm is already on its way toward land and the places of men.

# 5
# THE KILLER STRIKES

Even in its earliest, invisible form of a mere weather disturbance, the young storm was slowly being slid westward from its birthplace in the Atlantic's tropical waters. In that area, the "trade wind" belt, there is a constant east-to-west movement of the whole lower atmosphere, and the storm moves with it. Now that the hurricane is full-grown, its own winds give it an extra forward push.

Though the storm's winds are careening around its eye at upwards of a hundred miles an hour by now, the hurricane system as a whole—like an armored tank—takes some time to build up its forward speed. At first it rumbles across the sea at a leisurely twelve miles or so per hour. Its acceleration gradually increases until it may be stampeding headlong at as much as sixty miles an hour, faster than any armored tank charges into combat.

The hurricane does not advance in a straight line. Weathermen would be happier if it did; they'd know better where it was headed for, and what areas to warn of its approach. The ceaseless trade winds continue to help the storm along toward the west, but other external forces also influence the storm's direction. One of these, always present and always constant, is the earth's rotation. Just as it gives every wind a twist that makes it curve, so it gives the whole hurricane a nudge to the right that sends it gradually curving northward from its westerly course.*

Weathermen could still plot a hurricane's track in advance, allowing for the deflection of the earth's rotation, if that were the only force acting on it. But the hurricane's march is such a long one that it encounters other weather conditions in those thousands of miles, and reacts to every one of them. Sometimes it moves into the path of a fast following wind that hurries it along more rapidly than before, or subtly shifts its direction. Sometimes it bumps into a High of heavyweight cool air and, rather than plow its way right through that "hill" of high pressure, edges its way around it. Sometimes, at the height of the hurricane season, it may even collide with another hurricane. When that happens, the two of them ricochet away from each other, just the way two spinning marbles do when they hit.

As with so much else about the hurricane, there's a lot that is not known about the forces that push and steer it. Obviously they are many and various, because the hurricane often does queer things which cannot be accounted for. Sometimes it ignores the deflecting effect of the earth's rotation and *does* boom along in a perfectly straight line for a while, or even defies the force and bends southward, to the left, directly against the rotational impulsion. Sometimes it stops stockstill in its course—as the Last Island hurricane did—for hours or days before darting off at an angle to its former direction. Sometimes it will veer from its course and wander around in a loop or even a figure-eight before resuming its forward progress.

---

* Again, it's the opposite in the southern hemisphere. A typhoon off Australia would be deflected to the left of its course.

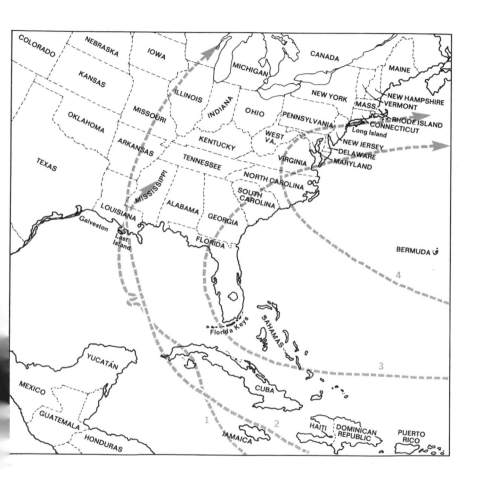

*These typical hurricane tracks show how the storm normally arrives on a westerly course, gradually turns northward, then "recurves" to the northeast. Track (1) is that of the Last Island hurricane of 1856; (2) a 1909 storm which killed 350 people in Cuba, Louisiana, and Mississippi; (3) the "Labor Day" hurricane that tore through the Florida Keys in 1935; and (4) hurricane Diane of 1955.*

Eventually, however, almost every hurricane and typhoon reaches land somewhere in its march. The first warning of the storm will probably be—as it was to the Last Islanders—the change in behavior of the incoming waves. On the beaches around the Gulf of Mexico, for instance, in ordinary weather twelve to fifteen waves scurry in to the sand every minute. When a hurricane is on the way, they slow to four or five waves per minute. They may start doing this a day or a week ahead of the storm, depending on how big the storm is and how much it is interfering with the sea's normal swell and movement. Another noticeable thing is that the day or two before a hurricane is often a spell of uncommonly beautiful weather, with unclouded skies and sparkling clean air.

The first sight of the storm itself will be some thin, filmy, ragged clouds radiating upward like a fan from a point somewhere below the horizon. The early Indian tribes in the Americas recognized these clouds as a portent of the hurricane, and taught the first Spanish explorers (who called the clouds *rabos de gallo,* "rooster tails") that the direction from which the clouds fanned was the direction from which the storm would come.

The rooster tails are composed of tiny ice crystals, and they are the first visible wisps of a tremendous "veil" overhanging the entire storm. This ice-crystal veil, the highest-flying and widest-spread cloud of the hurricane, has been condensed from the "exhaust" vapors spewed farthest into the sky by the storm's chimney. As the hurricane gets nearer, the veil covers most of the heavens, so that the sun or moon and stars, seen dimly through it, are sometimes ringed with halos. If the sun rises or sets behind the veil, there may be seen—as at Last Island—a brilliant but frightening display of grotesquely colored sky and sun.

Now there comes into view the rim of the hurricane's monster wheel of whirling cloud. It appears above the horizon of the sea like a rising mountain of dirty snow—a rounded hump, grayish-white in color. As the hump continues to rise, spreading wider and wider against the sky, its color darkens to gray, then dark gray,

*These tracks of "odd" hurricanes show that the storms can't always be depended upon to follow the "classic" curve, but may be wildly erratic— looping, zigzagging, even moving in a figure eight. Track (1) is that of the "Yankee" hurricane of 1935, the only one ever known to travel from north to south.*

then near-black, sometimes tinged with coppery red. This is known as the "bar" of the hurricane. If, as you watch, the bar seems to stay in the same place on the horizon, only increasing in height and width, the hurricane is moving directly toward you. If the bar slides slowly along the horizon like a moving mountain, the storm will pass to one side of you.

At the same time the "scud" arrives, the first flying shreds of cloud torn from the hurricane's pinwheel vanes. They are low-altitude clouds, and flutter across the sky at right angles to the veil and the rooster tails. If you are directly facing the storm, the scud (whirling, as you'll recall, counterclockwise around the storm's eye) will be blowing from your left to your right. You will feel the winds that blow them, too, and they come with a peculiar gustiness.

The wind increases in strength and flings quick showers of rain like handfuls of gravel. The sea is by now crashing onto the beach in tumultuous breakers. Very soon, both the wind and the rain are coming in a steady flow. The whole sky, the whole day darkens almost to midnight black as the main banks of cloud move overhead. The only light now comes from increasingly frequent jags of lightning. The rain becomes a downpour, the wind rises from gale force to storm force to hurricane force.

The damage done by the hurricane depends a good deal upon the direction from which it strikes, the time of day it arrives, and the physical contours of the land area it hits. Obviously, if the hurricane hits a town head-on, that town is going to be battered by the full force of the wind—perhaps blowing at 150 miles per hour—coming first from one side, then fading away in the lull of the eye, then blowing again as fiercely as before, but from the opposite side. However, a hurricane may have a diameter of as much as 250 miles. Some of the towns it assaults are not going to be hit head-on but brushed by either the left or the right rim of the hurricane's wheel.

The 150-m.p.h. wind is racing counterclockwise around the

*The Texas shore line begins to disappear under water as hurricane Beulah hurls its storm wave onto the palm-lined beaches of Corpus Christi.*
CORPUS CHRISTI CALLER

hurricane's eye and some segments of that wind are more dangerous than others. Suppose that the hurricane is being pushed by a 40-m.p.h. wind behind it. Around the right-hand edge of the storm's circle, its own wind of 150 m.p.h. is augmented by the 40-m.p.h. wind which is moving the whole storm system. In other words, the combined winds have an impact of 190 m.p.h. On the left-hand edge of the hurricane, however, its own wind is blowing backward against the wind that's pushing the storm. If the following wind's 40 m.p.h. is subtracted from the hurricane's 150 m.p.h., the effective wind force on that side is only 110 m.p.h. This is still a punishing, destroying, killing wind. But plainly, if there is *any* "safer" side to a hurricane, it is the left rather than the right. A hurricane with winds of 150 m.p.h. is "one of the big ones." But how big the biggest storms are—in terms of wind speed—is unknown. To measure wind velocity, a weather bureau has to poke an instrument called an anemometer up into the wind itself, and in the fiercer storms the instrument gets blown to pieces or blown away entirely. Anemometers in various storms have recorded wind speeds well in excess of 150 m.p.h.—some have reached 180 m.p.h.—before they broke down or disappeared, so the wind velocity was obviously much faster than was recorded in each case.

After several especially destructive hurricanes, engineers have examined the damage done to structures which they knew were built to withstand certain extreme stresses, and have concluded that the wind had to have reached at least 200 miles per hour to have destroyed them. So, although weather experts generally say that hurricanes "can" reach 200-m.p.h. speeds, and typhoons "can" exceed 250 m.p.h., the storms' maximum speed is still incalculable.

It is hard to comprehend, without experiencing it, just how strong and fierce a hurricane wind is. A physics textbook can say that a 150-m.p.h. wind exerts a pressure of approximately 112 pounds on every square foot of surface it blows against. But the bare figures can't tell what that feels like. A man simply could not stand against it; he would be whisked away like a leaf. Even if a man of medium size, weighing 160 pounds, were to throw himself flat on the ground, his head to the wind, he'd still be blown away. Even in that position, his head and shoulders would present a surface area of about a square foot and a half, against which the wind would slam with an impact of 168 pounds, more than the man's weight. He would be shoved along the ground—slowly at first, but irresistibly—scraping and grinding, then bouncing and bounding like a tumbleweed.

In a 150-m.p.h. wind, even the smallest house, a box ten feet high and twenty feet long, would have its windward side hit with a weight of more than eleven tons. That's not a random gust that hits and runs. The hurricane wind is so steady and long-blowing that those eleven tons his the house and lean there against it like a bulldozer. At the same time, there is a "negative pressure" on the other side of the house. Where the wind blows past the building's lee side, it leaves a pocket of partial vacuum that sucks almost as powerfully as the storm is pushing on the windward wall. Few structures can resist such a remorseless dual attack. Even if a house does survive, its supports are weakened, bent, or cracked;

*Only the steeple of this church in central Texas was left standing, after hurricane Beulah roared over it in 1967.*

*ESSA*

when the leading edge of the hurricane passes and its trailing edge brings a wind smashing from the opposite direction, the house usually can stand no more, and crashes down.

Structures built of solid concrete might seem to be indestructible, but they are vulnerable to the killer storm in a special way. Remember: that 150-m.p.h. wind is also loaded with tons of water. And so *very* strong is the wind that it can force the water deep into the concrete so that its chemical composition becomes crumbly and soft. Like a sugar cube being sprayed, the concrete can literally dissolve.

The winds' uproar is the most terrifying aspect of the storm. The winds flatten farm crops and forests and houses; they hurl deadly missiles about—tree branches or whole trees, debris and broken glass from blown-down buildings, even heavy automobiles—and they do kill people in one way or another. But, for all their destructiveness, the winds actually do the *least* harm of any of the hurricane's weapons. They rank third as a damage-doer, behind the rain and the storm wave. (In Florida, the United States' most hurricane-harried state, insurance against wind damage can be bought quite cheaply, but no insurance company will insure property against flood or wave damage, except perhaps if an extortionate premium on the policy is paid.)

Weathermen in the United States are accustomed to refer to a rain as "light" if less than one tenth of an inch of water falls during one hour. They call it "moderate" if an hour's rainfall measures between one tenth and three tenths of an inch. It's a "heavy" rain if it piles up more than three tenths of an inch in an hour. What then should they call a rainfall that spills more than *one and a half inches* of water per hour, and hammers down for twenty-four hours without let-up, leaving a total of thirty-eight inches of water on the ground? That's what one hurricane poured onto the town of Thrall, Texas, in 1921.

The rain that falls during a storm is nowhere near so dramatic or frightening as the clamorous wind and blinding lightning. But just an average, ordinary hurricane may dump between five and ten inches of rain onto each area it passes. To give an idea of what this means: *one inch* of rain covering one single city block weighs one hundred and sixty *tons*. One inch of rain on a square mile of countryside weighs 32,000 tons.

That is far too much water for even the thirstiest earth to absorb, or for the ordinary channels of run-off to cope with, but that water must go somewhere. In the city it floods cellars, clogs sewers, rises in the streets to inundate parked cars. In the country it sets streams foaming over their banks into farm fields and barnyards. In mountainous areas it cuts loose avalanches and mudslides. However, the downpour's immediate effects are not its worst. Long after the hurricane has passed, *all* the water it dumped onto thousands of square miles of land may drain off into the few rivers in that area, make them overflow their usual watercourses, and send great surging floods downstream to devastate communities which perhaps had not even felt the original storm.

But the hurricane's most terrible and most immediate destroyer comes from the sea. All the time the storm has been crossing open water it has been heaping up before it a "storm wave"—or, more accurately, a whole series of them, each wave shoving another ahead of it, and the hurricane herding the whole flock. These waves, like the winds that heap them up, are heavier and more tumultuous on the right-hand edge of the storm wheel. There they may reach heights of seventy feet—higher than a five-storey building. Higher, too, than the ground on which many of our coastal cities stand.

In addition to the towering storm waves, the hurricane is also carrying along a minor mountain of ocean inside its eye. The air pressure is so low in there, where the chimney updraft is sucking upward, that the ocean level rises inside it just the way liquid rises into a straw. This traveling circle of sea does not bulge perceptibly; its level may be no more than a foot higher than the ocean elsewhere. But the average hurricane's eye is fifteen miles in diameter. When it's lifting a foot-high amount of water, that water weighs

*After hurricane Betsy in 1965, a Salvation Army "mobile canteen" splashes through a flooded Louisiana street, on its way to provide emergency meals for the storm's victims.*

SALVATION ARMY

as much as a small mountain—more than four and a half billion tons—and the storm is carrying it along at a speed of perhaps sixty miles an hour.

Imagine that the hurricane is charging directly into a U-shaped bay, and at the inner bend of the U is a seaport city. The port is already considerably damaged, because lesser waves stirred up by the storm's approach have been crowding into the harbor for hours or days before. They have tossed all the anchored boats about, and dashed them against one another, and have torn and smashed at the piers and breakwaters and seaside streets of the city.

Now comes the hurricane. It is accompanied by those monstrous waves, five storeys tall, far overtopping the city's saewall. They pile into the bay, one behind another. Meanwhile, the hurricane's winds have been playing hob with the bay's original content of water, scooping that up into the bend of the U. So what now advances on the city is the wind-whipped water that was already in the bay, and behind that the awful rank upon rank of storm waves, and behind them the mountainous weight of water riding in the storm's eye.

Impelled by a wind of 150 miles per hour, the waves roll with the speed of express trains. The first moving cliff of water crashes against the city's seawall, flinging spray high into the air. (Spray may not be all that it flings. A storm wave's breaking surf hits with a force of three tons to the square inch. It has been known to hurl large stones through the windows of lighthouses 300 feet above the sea.) After the thunderous breaking crash, those million-or-so tons of salt water hump up and over the seawall, into the low-lying streets. Before that wave has time to slosh back into the bay, another wave is racing in behind it. And another and another, each surge heaping higher and heavier atop the waters that arrived before. There is nowhere for them to go except farther up into the bend of the bay's U, and nothing that stands in the way—walls, buildings, dikes, emergency barriers—nothing stands for long.

It may seem that the storm wave could hardly be any worse than it has just been described. But it can be, if it happens to arrive in that bay at the time of day when the bay waters are at their natural high tide. The gravitational pull of the moon (and, to a lesser degree, the sun) raises these tides twice a day along the world's seashores. In many places along America's coastline the high tides lift the local sea level as much as eighteen feet above low tide. Obviously, if the sea is already lapping at the highwater mark on a city's seawall, the hurricane's added storm wave is going to be that much more calamitous.

The amount of the storm's damage can also depend in part

on the physical shape of the land mass it hits. Conditions are grim enough when a storm wave pours into a U-shaped bay, but suppose it were V-shaped. In the U, the waters race unimpeded down its broad expanse and slop over at its closed end. In the V, the waters heap up higher from the moment they enter its narrowing arms, and sluice along faster, exactly as if they were being poured through a funnel.

Precisely those conditions made an Indian Ocean typhoon, in 1737, the most murderous killer storm in all of history. It slammed its storm waves into the V-shaped Bay of Bengal. The Bay is a roomy 800 miles wide where its V opens into the ocean, but the shores of India and Burma on each side narrow it sharply down to a point at the delta of the Ganges River.

The typhoon's wave may not have been spectacular when it first washed between the arms of the V, but it gained height, weight, and speed as the narrowing banks crammed it together. In its swoop down the Bay, the wave mowed it clean of everything afloat. Fully twenty thousand vessels, ranging in size from little fishing hoys to ocean-going Blackwall frigates, disappeared into and under the frothing juggernaut of the wave.

Long before the wave reached the point of the V, the Bay was no longer V-shaped. The sea waters burst over the shores and seethed over a land area the size of the state of Massachusetts. Four large and heavily populated islands in the Bay, each of them twice the size of New York's Manhattan Island, disappeared entirely until the waters eventually receded. More than 300,000 people died. Only two other natural disasters recorded since the world began have ever snuffed out so many human lives at one blow.*

The hurricane occasionally brings still another menace. Like a shark being followed by scavenger fish which feed on its leftovers, the killer storm is often accompanied by one or more of the smaller but equally vicious storms called tornadoes.

* A flood in China in 1887 killed some 900,000 people. An earthquake in 1556, also in China, took 830,000 lives.

The tornado is nicknamed by some weathermen "the hurricane's kid sister," which makes it sound merely mischievous. It is decidedly more than that, as we shall see in a later chapter. It is enough to say here that the tornado is a killer, too, a storm of pure wind and cloud, shaped like a long funnel or hose extending from cloud to earth. Where the hurricane works its destruction like a giant bull-dozer, scraping the whole face of the earth, the tornado acts more like the nozzle of a giant vacuum cleaner, scouring a narrower path.

*Another scene of Betsy's aftermath in Louisiana shows rescue boats floating alongside flood-installed automobiles.*

*ESSA*

Either one of these killer storms is bad enough by itself. But often a hurricane will have one or several tornadoes dangling from the outer edges of its cloud wheel, or else its passing will leave the local weather conditions somehow favorable for the formation of tornadoes. So an already bruised and bloodied population may be further battered.

One remaining hurricane "weapon" is its eye. This calm, rain-free, often cloudless, even sunny space in the storm's center usually comes as a welcome breather between the storm's two rake-overs. But it, too, can be unpleasant, and sometimes do some minor damage of its own.

The temperature of the surrounding storm is generally about 75° Fahrenheit, quite a comfortable temperature. But as the eye arrives the temperature can shoot up abruptly to 90°F., while the humidity drops just as suddenly. After the warm wetness of the storm, this unexpectedly hot, dry air seems actually to burn the skin. Also, the air's abnormally low pressure can make one's ears pop uncomfortably, and even burst the tiny blood vessels in the back of the throat, causing a taste of blood in the mouth or a trickle of nosebleed. In the partial vacuum of the eye's low air pressure, a tightly shut-up building, whose inside air is at a more normal pressure, may blow out all its windows, providing more ammunition for the next wind to throw.

The main menace of the eye is the false impression it gives that "the storm is all over." The natives of the West Indies had a hard time convincing their first European visitors that this sudden calm was *not* the end of the bad weather but just a gap. The Europeans who didn't believe them soon regretted it. But even in modern times the eye still deceives the unwary.

A hurricane that hit Miami, Florida, in September, 1926, besieged the city all during a day and a night. Toward dawn the winds gentled down. People crept from their shelters to see how much of Miami was still standing. Some of them walked out onto the long causeway that crosses Biscayne Bay between the mainland city and Miami Beach, to watch the massive waves that were still pounding through the normally tranquil Bay. Some of the people crossed to Miami Beach for the challenge of swimming in the ocean's now-thundering surf.

The eye took just one hour to cross the city, and it was the last hour of life for all those Miamians who had been foolish enough to trust the calm. Sightseers were still sauntering along the causeway and crowds of thrill-seekers were on the beach when the storm's second blast came. The ocean literally swallowed the beach and all the bathers on it. The Bay waters reached up to sweep the causeway clean. Hundreds of people died, needlessly.

More recently, in September, 1967, when a hurricane hit the Texas coast, only ten deaths were reported. But one of the victims was a 15-year-old girl, who was tempted by the eye's deceptive calm to try her surfboard on the towering waves after the storm had "gone."

Once a hurricane leaves the sea for the land, it is doomed to die, sooner or later. The hurricane encounters more friction on the contoured solid land than it did on the smooth, liquid sea, and that slows both its whirling winds and its forward movement. The friction, however, is only one factor, and a minor one, in the eventual death of the killer storm. What mainly kills it is starvation, from a lack of energy fuel.

The hurricane requires both heat and moisture to stay alive, and the surface of the ground provides far less of both than the ocean does. Not even every ocean is warm enough to fuel the storm's energy engine. The few hurricanes which form off the west coast of Mexico or Baja California usually live very short lives, because their northward path through the Pacific soon brings them over the chill waters of the California Current, too cold to keep them going. Any storm that wanders away from the warm, wide waters that gave it birth is forced to feed on its reserve store of energy. As that diminishes, so does its strength.

But a big enough hurricane, with a big enough reserve of energy, may take a long time to die. A storm crashing from out of the Atlantic onto the coast of Florida begins to lose force the moment it plows inland, but it can often survive long enough to cross the peninsula and reach the Gulf of Mexico. There, finding new supplies of heat and moisture, it can build up again, perhaps even stronger than before, and move on across the Gulf to bludgeon some other shore. Several hurricanes, traveling north along the Atlantic seaboard, have smashed inland at various places, and each time dodged back out to sea as if deliberately to refuel before making a fresh assault on the land.

A 1966 storm began its career in mid-August over West Africa as a low-pressure area of weather "disturbance." It moved slowly westward and, after it passed the Cape Verde Islands, it became a full-sized hurricane. At that point it came to the notice of an orbiting weather satellite, which kept an eye on its entire further career. The hurricane bowled on across the Atlantic, brushed through the outer islands of the West Indies, then, in the vicinity of Haiti, began to edge to the northward. It followed almost precisely the curve of the United States' east coastline, though staying some 200 miles out at sae. At about the latitude of New York City it swung more to the east and cruised up and across the whole of the North Atlantic.

When it reached the Norwegian Sea it was directly north of its original starting point in Africa (but some 3,500 miles north of it), and there it began to lose force, deteriorating into just a weather "disturbance" again. But it still packed plenty of wind and rain as it crossed the peninsula of Norway, Sweden, and Finland. Over the northern reaches of Russia, it turned directly north through the Barents Sea into the Arctic Ocean, and finally died in mid-September, of heat and moisture starvation, in the neighborhood of the North Pole, on the other side of the earth from its birthplace.

That hurricane was not a real killer. It spent little time over land areas (which accounts for the long duration of activity) and it did little damage except to a couple of ships at sea. But it lived for a month, crossed the Atlantic Ocean twice, went farther north than any other hurricane known to history, and traveled some 15,000 miles during its career. All told, that was probably the longest journey ever made and the longest life ever lived by a hurricane.

# 6
# THE BAD, THE GOOD, AND THE ODD

"Eyes never beheld the seas so high, angry and covered by foam," wrote the admiral in his journal after the hurricane had passed. For a day and a night he had not dared to leave the quarterdeck of his imperilled flagship. But now the storm had finally abated, his fleet was safe, and he had come below to his cabin to write a report of the event.

"The wind not only prevented our progress, but offered no opportunity to run behind any headland for shelter; hence we were forced to keep out in this bloody ocean, seething like a pot on a hot fire. Never did the sky look more terrible; for one whole day and night it blazed like a furnace; the flashes came with such fury and frightfulness that we all thought the ships would be blasted. All this time the water never ceased to fall from the sky; I don't say 'it rained,' because it was like another Deluge."

That might have been written by any naval officer in any recent hurricane season, but it was done nearly five centuries ago, and the admiral who wrote it was Christopher Columbus. It was the first written eyewitness description of a West Indies hurricane.

The West Indies and other parts of America had been mauled by numberless hurricanes during the millenniums before then, but the native inhabitants of the West Indies had no written language and left no records of the weather. The European explorers and settlers who arrived after Columbus didn't keep very complete weather records either, but they did at least leave some accounts. Those early voyagers' comments were often more dramatic than descriptive, as when the scientist-priest, Father du Tertre, wrote of the hurricanes he encountered during his travels through America in the 1600's: "They are the most horrible and violent tempests one can name, true pictures of the final fire and destruction of the world." Sometimes the accounts were no more than appalled gasps. "My God! to think that the wind could have such force!" wrote a Lieutenant Archer, an officer aboard the British warship H.M.S. *Phoenix,* after surviving a hurricane in 1780.

Sometimes the newcomers condensed what they had learned about the killer storms into weather proverbs and sayings. For example, the Negro slaves in the Bahamas memorized the months of the hurricane season with a calypso jingle:

> June: too soon
> July: stand by
> August: look out you must
> September: remember
> October: all over

This is more or less correct for the Bahama Islands, where July, August, and September are the likeliest months for a hurricane to appear. The jingle doesn't hold true for the rest of the Americas. In 1968 the month of June ("too soon") brought three full-blown hurricanes to the Gulf of Mexico and the Caribbean Sea. In 1893 the month of October ("all over") brought a hurricane that drowned 1,800 people along the Texas and Louisiana coasts. In other years, an occasional out-of-season hurricane has come along as early as January and as late as December.

The early American weather reports, while they may have been accurate enough in a short-sighted sort of way, sometimes were combined to give an overall weather picture that was quite misleading. In 1780, for instance, practically every ship and every island in the western Atlantic and the Carribean suffered the attack of a hurricane. When the several ships' masters and the islands' governors compared notes afterward, they discovered that they had all been hit at just about the same time. They wrote letters about it to their relatives, employers, or government superiors in Europe. For fifty years afterward, in both America and Europe, the storm was referred to as the Great Hurricane, not the "great hurricane of 1780" nor the "great West Indian hurricane," just *the* Great Hurricane.

Then, half a century later, historians studying the ships' logs and colonial archives of that time found that the victims' accounts of the storm varied in such major details as the direction the storm was traveling. Eventually they unraveled the contradictory stories and determined that there hadn't been one hurricane but three, all in that area at the same time. No one of the three had been outstandingly severe; the Great Hurricane turned out to have been just a great coincidence.

All the early accounts of hurricanes and typhoons leave out a great deal. During the span of three hundred years from Admiral Columbus down to Lieutenant Archer, every voyager who encountered a killer storm described it in much the same way: "My God, how awful!" He would tell how frightening the storm was, and how frightened *he* was, but he'd be vague about what the storm actually did that was so awful. We are accustomed today to hearing every hurricane described in terms of the number of lives it takes and the number of dollars' worth of property it damages, so it may seem odd that the early chroniclers so seldom mentioned any wholesale slaughter or extensive destruction.

The reason is that, in those times, there wasn't very much for a killer storm *to* damage. In 1635, a century and a half after America's discovery, when a hurricane slashed north through New Sweden, New Amsterdam, and the Plymouth Colony (New Jersey, New York, and Massachusetts), the worst damage reported was the "widespread destruction of trees." Three centuries after Columbus, the American population was still sparse and scattered, and the towns were few and small. In the whole of the United States, in 1790, there were less than four million people. The nation's capital and largest city, Philadelphia, had only 40,000 inhabitants.

On the other side of the world there wasn't much either, in those days, for a typhoon to demolish. Most of the Pacific islands were sparsely inhabited. China and Japan were civilized, but they had long ago learned to build their cities of flimsy and easily replaceable materials—because when a typhoon wasn't tearing them down, an earthquake was.

Through all the years before the nineteenth century, the only killer storms that were widely noticed outside their immediate areas of devastation were those that interfered with the course of history, like the hurricane that scattered the Spanish Armada in 1588; those that took a really horrendous toll of lives, like the Bay of Bengal typhoon in 1737; those that were sensational freaks (or were believed to be), like the Great Hurricane of 1780; and those few that devastated a large and populous city.

One historic killer storm that blew some good, in an odd and roundabout way, was a hurricane that hit the city of St. Croix in the Virgin Islands in 1772. A 15-year-old boy, an apprentice clerk in a counting-house there, wrote a letter about the storm to his father on another island. It read, in part:

"Good God! What horror and destruction—it is impossible for me to describe or you to form any idea of it. The roaring of the sea and wind—fiery meteors flying about in the air—the prodigious glare of almost perpetual lightning—the crash of the falling houses—and the ear-piercing shrieks of the distressed were sufficient to strike astonishment into Angels . . .''

The boy's father was so proud of the letter that he showed it to friends, and one of them sent it on to the editor of the St. Croix *Gazette,* where it was published. The newspaper's readers were also impressed. Some of them, rich planters on the island, thought the young writer showed such promise that he deserved a chance at higher education, and they collected a fund to send him to college in New York City. The boy was a brilliant student; within five years, by the age of twenty, he had become confidential secretary to General George Washington. Eventually he became one of the "founding fathers" of the United States, one of the authors of the new nation's Constitution, and the first Secretary of its Treasury. He might even have become President, except that he was disqualified for the office by having been born outside the country's borders. His name was Alexander Hamilton.

From about the year 1800 on, more and more killer storms were reported, not just the outstanding ones, and the reports were much more detailed about their behavior and destructiveness. This was not because the storms were getting either more numerous or more violent. It was because people were getting more numerous in the storm areas.

By the start of the nineteenth century, there were European colonies all over the globe. In what had formerly been blank spots on the map marked "unexplored," there were now outposts and settlements. Where there had been frontier stockades, there were now towns. Every sea was crisscrossed with a busy traffic of ships. Where once a hurricane or a typhoon might have trampled through a wilderness without a soul knowing of its existence, there were now people to suffer from it and to lose their property to it.

In some places—Last Island is an example—a killer storm might demolish a community so thoroughly that its inhabitants

*Manhattan's streets stream with water after hurricane Donna, in September of 1960, brought a ten-foot storm wave across the island, the highest tide waters ever recorded in New York City's history.*

*AMERICAN RED CROSS*

would be discouraged from ever building there again. More likely, though, the survivors of such a storm would staunchly rebuild, and usually they would put up a bigger and better community than before. So the town would then attract even more residents, with the result that, if another storm struck the same place, the death toll and damages would be even greater. Thus the weather records of a hurricane-prone territory may seem to indicate that the storms are getting worse every time they attack.

In 1635 a storm careened from New Jersey into New England with no more effect than a "widespread destruction of trees." In 1815, a hurricane of approximately the same size followed almost the identical path. It killed about two dozen people and did an estimated half million dollars' worth of damage. In 1938, still another hurricane of similar size roared along the same track. It killed 548 people and destroyed about 300 million dollars' worth of property.

Most of the storms that made their mark on the pages of history since 1800 have left a black mark indeed, commemorating the havoc and horror they wrought. But others have been remembered for the oddness of their behavior or the curious, rather than calamitous, effects they caused. A few have merited notice for the good they did along with the bad. Among these is the 1818 hurricane of Texas which sank four of the buccaneer Jean Laffite's pirate ships.

The very last year of the nineteenth century was marked by the most *killing* killer storm that has ever hit the United States: the infamous Galveston hurricane of 1900.

Galveston is a Texas island on the Gulf of Mexico, thirty miles long but only four miles across at its widest point. It lies athwart the entrance to Galveston Bay, one of Texas' busiest seaports. Besides being the rampart to this harbor, the island is also a popular resort; it is lined with beautiful beaches and laden with subtropical flowers. The city, also named Galveston, which occupies one end of the island, had a population of about 20,000 in the year 1900, but it was crowded with an additional unknown number of vacationers and tourists on September 8, the day the hurricane hit.

Galveston is hot in summer, so at that time most of the houses in the city were built low, rambling, and flat-roofed, with a layer of loose crushed rock spread on the roofs to deflect the blazing sun. When the hurricane wind came, it seized up all those acres of rocks—the size of eggs, but jagged—and fired them through the city like bursts of shrapnel. As usual, though, the storm wave was the chief assassin. It reared up and over and crashed down, across the entire island. Fully half of the city's buildings and houses— three thousand of them—were swept off into Galveston Bay. A large ocean steamer moored off the island was pitched all the way through the Bay, up onto the Texas mainland, and stranded on dry ground a mile from the normal waterside.

There are many poignant stories told about that historic storm. When the storm had subsided and rescue parties started picking through the wreckage, a baby was found nailed to what was left of a house roof. A spike had been driven through its tiny wrist and into the roof's wooden rafters. Someone—probably its frantic parents—had done that in a last desperate attempt to save the child from being washed away and certainly drowned. And the pitiful attempt worked; the baby lived.

The Galveston hurricane butchered more people than have ever been killed in one American locality in one day, excepting the casualties in some of the Civil War battles. At least six thousand people died; some estimates range as high as eight thousand. There are four grim reasons why the exact death toll at Galveston will never be known. One, because so many victims simply vanished, hurled right off the island. Two, because so many of the bodies that were found were too badly torn up to be identified. Three, because there is no knowing how many visiting vacationers were on the island. And four—the most grotesque horror of all—because the storm scraped open the city's cemetery, smashed the coffins, and tumbled already-dead bodies among those it had newly killed.

After the hurricane, Galveston determined that such a catastrophe should never happen again. It built a seawall, stout and thick and ten feet high, along seventeen miles of the island's Gulf front. When the next hurricane came that way, in 1915, its winds did considerable damage on the island and killed 275 people, but the devastating storm wave was successfully kept out. The city, exposed as it is to the many storms that blow out of the Gulf, would not be there at all if it weren't for the protecting wall. That still stands, and so does Galveston.

A far worse disaster, in Japan, is still referred to as the "Great Earthquake" of 1923, and not many history books record that a typhoon was partly responsible for the devastation. When the cataclysm was over, the cities of Tokyo and Yokohama were rubble and ashes, more than 99,000 people were dead, nearly half that number were missing and never found, and more than 100,000 were injured. The earth tremor itself did not actually hurt many people, because Japan at that time didn't have many tall or solidly-

*At the height of 1960's hurricane Donna's attack on North Carolina's Outer Banks, its storm wave begins to surge into the marina of a small coastal town.*
*AMERICAN RED CROSS*

built buildings to be toppled. What caused most of the death and damage was a raging fire. It was started when the earthquake jostled stoves and spilled cooking fires. It was fed by the wood-and-paper construction of most of the houses, and it was fanned into fury by the winds of the typhoon.

The Japanese had known that the typhoon was coming up the Pacific coast of the islands, and had battened down for the blow. The first fringe of the storm brushed Yokohama, and people there remarked that it was an unusual one; it brought high winds but almost no rain. Then the earthquake rocked both Yokohama and the adjoining city of Tokyo. By the time the people had recovered from the shock, both cities were speckled with hundreds of separate fires. Before anything could be done about them, the typhoon's still-rainless winds had fanned them into one all-devouring conflagration.

The entire population of both cities fled for their lives—in trucks, buses, ox-carts, jinrickishas, on foot—into the wind and away from the roaring flames. They might have escaped, and the death toll might have been much less, except—again—for the killer storm. Its eye passed over the area during that mass stampede. With its passing, the wind changed and blew the fire in exactly the opposite direction. Like a flood of flame, it chased and caught and churned right over the mobs of fleeing people, and incinerated them.

Several scientists have speculated that the typhoon might have been more than the earthquake's partner in this frightful disaster; they suggest that the typhoon may have helped to *cause* the earthquake. The islands of Japan lie along a geological fault, a crack in the planet's crust where the earth masses on either side are jammed face to face under terrific and uneasy tension. When the tension occasionally becomes too great and unequal, these masses slip and grind together, and that's an earthquake. It is not impossible that the impact of a killer storm could add just the stress that would cause the earth masses to shift.

Japan's geological fault runs along the bottom of the deep Pacific ocean, already under an incalculable weight of water and far below the wind and waves kicked up by a typhoon. But one scientist, C. F. Brooks, has estimated that a ten-foot rise of water in a storm wave would add about nine million tons of weight to each square mile of the sea bottom. At the same time, the storm's lowered air pressure would remove some two million tons of the air normally resting on each square mile of exposed land area. If his theory is sound, that abrupt imbalance, the land suddenly lighter on one side of the fault, the sea heavier on the other side, could trigger a shift along the fault and a quake of the earth's surface above.

There are many instances of how a killer storm can cause repercussions far beyond its immediate area of operation. When a hurricane hit Miami in 1926, it did a fantastic amount of destruction in that city, and also, in a sense, wrecked the whole state of Florida for a while.

Most of the state had been an undeveloped waste of swamps and scrub forest until shortly after World War I, when it enjoyed a land boom. Developers started draining the swamps, erecting ambitious young cities like Miami, and selling property at ever-higher prices, both to new settlers who swarmed into the state and to northern speculators who had never seen Florida. By 1926 the state seemed like a Promised Land of plenty and prosperity.

Then the hurricane busted the boom. It drowned all the people —most of them presumably newcomers and unacquainted with hurricanes—who poured out onto Miami's causeway and Miami Beach during the eye's calm interval. The storm also drove an excursion steamer from Biscayne Bay into the middle of the city. Then it *bent* Miami's newest and proudest skyscraper—the 14-storey Myer-Kiser Bank Building—knocking it fifteen degrees off the vertical. The building had to be torn down. The marooned ship was too big to be moved, so the city converted it into an aquarium, in hopes that it would prove a tourist attraction. However, it and the rest of Miami and the whole of Florida didn't attract much of anything or anybody for a long time afterward. The new settlers who had been drawn by the land boom were repelled by the hurricane; they packed up and fled. The out-of-state speculators yanked out the money they had invested. The boom collapsed, the developers lost fortunes, and much of Florida sank back into its former swampy stagnation.

Later attempts to revive the boom were thwarted by recurrent new storms. In 1928, a hurricane somehow avoided damaging Florida's coastal areas, but moved inland and swept straight across Lake Okeechobee. This vast body of water is the second-largest freshwater lake within the United States' borders. It covers an area of some 750 square miles, but a man can wade across it almost anywhere without getting his nose underwater. Its deepest spots are only fifteen feet deep.

In 1928 there were several thousand people living around Okeechobee's shores: small farmers, fishermen, trappers, and the like. They had ample warning of the hurricane's approach, but about all they did was to shutter their cabin windows against the expected high winds. They simply never gave a thought to Lake Okeechobee and its warm, shallow, unruffled waters. But those waters, just because they *were* shallow, were easily picked up by the hurricane blast. Like a rubber squeegee wiping a wet windowpane, the storm came from one side of the lake, rolled up the water before it, and emptied it out the other side, onto all the little farm communities and cabin towns. Shallow though the lake was, its content of water weighed something like eight billion tons.

In one hour, 1,836 of the people living around Lake Okeechobee were living no longer. Nearly another two thousand were injured. Most of the victims died by drowning, but a number of them died of snakebite. When the lakeside dwellers realized that they were being inundated, many of them tried to clamber into trees and climb above the flood crest. But they found that hordes of venomous water moccasins, also fleeing, were already twined and coiled among the branches.

On Labor Day of 1935, yet another hurricane tore into Florida, and weathermen rate this as the most ferocious storm ever to hit the American mainland, with winds of 200 miles per hour and perhaps higher. This one raged through the Keys, that string of islands which trails off the peninsula's southern tip. Another of Florida's hopeful but ill-fated "developments" was in progress there: a railroad being built from the mainland to run across the islands to the last one in the chain, Key West. Again there was plenty of advance warning, and the workers strung out along the rail line were alerted to expect a special train that would pick them all up and take them to the mainland.

But, for some reason, the train started out too late to beat the storm. Many of the workers were caught by the hurricane while they waited on the shelterless and low-lying Keys. Then the rescue train was trapped, when a trestle between two of the islands, which it had just crossed, was blown down behind it. More than four hundred people died in that storm, and so many over-water stretches of the railroad were smashed that the project was abandoned. (Later, a more solidly-constructed motor highway was built instead.)

By this time, people in the northern states, having heard all about these several disasters, had stopped referring to the storms as "West Indian hurricanes" (which had formerly been their popular name), and weren't even saying just plain "hurricanes." Now people called them *"Florida* hurricanes."

However, in that same year of 1935, another hurricane was born—in the North Atlantic near Bermuda, where no such storm had been known to originate before. Defying all the laws of physics and normal hurricane behavior, it swooped from north to south, passed the Carolinas and Georgia, made an abrupt sideways turn and plowed across the Florida peninsula. Fortunately, it traversed a fairly uninhabited area, so it took no lives and did little damage. Now Floridians were able to twit their hecklers up north by dubbing this extraordinary storm "the *Yankee* hurricane."

Three years later, the Yankees up north really did have a killer storm of their own, the "great New England hurricane" of September, 1938. The northeastern United States had been hit by such storms before, but this was the area's first big one in the twentieth

century, the first big one since the area had become heavily populated and industrialized.

Because New England hadn't suffered such a storm since the
1800's—which no one living remembered—the people in that part
of the country regarded hurricanes rather as they might have regarded Indian raids: something that used to happen but didn't any
more. Even when the weather bureaus convinced them that a hurricane was indeed on its way, the New Englanders could not
imagine what a fury it would be. Their preparations for it were
only half-hearted—and half-cheerful, as if they were in for an
unusual entertainment.

Some entertainment. Five hundred and forty-eight people dead or
missing, three hundred million dollars' worth of property smashed,
vanished, gone. As the storm churned north along the coast of New
Jersey, its eye was thirty miles offshore, but its left-side winds and
rain pounded the whole length of the state. Then, while that same
left edge battered New York City, the full front of the storm
crashed into Long Island like a runaway truck hitting a stone wall.
The storm waves were thirty to forty feet high, and most of the
118-mile-long island is no higher than that.

Scientists had often been told, by West Indian natives, that they
had felt their whole island shake when a killer storm's wave hit it.
The scientists had always smiled tolerantly and ignored such
yarns; they felt sure that the "ground shaking" was only an impression created by terror and imagination; they knew that waves
of water could not jostle any sizeable piece of solid land. The scientists don't smile at such stories any longer. When the 1938 storm
waves thundered against Long Island, the seismographic instruments in the department of earthquake studies at Fordham Uni-
versity—sixty-five miles away in New York City—jittered and
jiggled just as if they were registering the shocks of an actual earthquake.

What happened to the town of Westhampton on the south shore
of Long Island is typical of the fate of many other towns and vil-

lages on that island. Westhampton consisted of 150 buildings before the hurricane came; immediately afterward, it had six. When the storm finished mowing down almost every standing object on Long Island, it leaped across the Sound and hurled itself into the mainland of New England.

It was now moving at an exceptionally fast forward speed— more than fifty miles per hour—too fast for the weather bureaus in cities along the way to anticipate its track before it hit them. A radio station might be broadcasting the frantic warning that "the hurricane is on its way here" at the same moment that the storm was toppling the station's transmitter tower and putting it off the air. As an example of how the hurricane caught its victims by surprise: in Providence, Rhode Island, people were lounging around in seeming safety in the lobbies of midtown hotels when the storm wave came roaring up the twenty miles of Narragansett Bay, into the city, through the hotels' revolving doors, and drowned the people there among the potted palms.

The final statistics: 448 people died (their bodies were found and identified); 100 are still listed as "missing" (they vanished utterly, and can be presumed dead); 1,754 more were injured; 1,991 homes were demolished, and so were 4,974 commercial buildings; 6,933 summer houses in the vacation resorts along the coast were destroyed; 2,605 boats were sunk or lost; a total of 93,122 families were affected, either by a death or injury in the family, or by being rendered homeless, or by suffering such destitution that they had to live on emergency welfare money for a time.

After the hurricane had savaged its way through all of New England and gone off to die in mid-Canada, the survivors breathed a sigh of relief, as if to say, "Well, that's over; it'll be our grandchildren who see the next one." But a few people looked up the old weather records. In the previous century, New England's worst hurricane had occurred in 1815, and had been followed by one almost as bad six years later, in 1821. These few cautious people wondered if possibly history might repeat itself.

*These two photographs, taken in 1960 at two separate locales in Florida, show hurricane Donna's effect on the mobile homes in a trailer court and the cabins of a beachside motel.* ✓

AMERICAN RED CROSS

Sure enough, just six years later to the month, in September of 1944, another hurricane boomed up through the Atlantic, following almost mile for mile the same course as the "great one" of 1938. This time, as people prepared for its onslaught, no one treated it as a lark. This time, since they *were* scared and safely under cover, only forty-six of them fell victim to the storm.

Also, the property damage it did was merely a third as great. As it reached New England, the storm veered just slightly eastward, to the right, so the fiercer winds—and the bulk of the storm wave—stayed farther out to sea, while the mainland got the comparatively milder winds of the storm's left-hand segment. However, the portion of the hurricane that hung out over the sea was still lethal. September, 1944, was the middle of World War II, and both the U.S. Navy and Coast Guard had ships cruising off New England. Five of them went down: a destroyer, two cutters, a lightship, and a minesweeper, and took 298 sailors with them.

In 1950, by which time the U.S. Weather Bureau was watching every hurricane that blew up anywhere in the western hemisphere, the Bureau found that it was often tracking two or more storms at a time, so it started giving them separate names in order to tell them apart. Naming hurricanes was nothing new. Men had always remembered the more disastrous ones by some title like "the great New England hurricane," or by naming them after a notable ship that was lost in the storm ("the *Racer's* hurricane"), and the Roman Catholic peoples of Latin America were accustomed to naming a storm after the saint on whose memorial day it arrived.

At first, the Weather Bureau designated the storms by letters of the alphabet. Later it used the "military alphabet"—Able for A, Baker for B, Charlie, Dog, Easy, Fox, and so on. That turned out to be confusing, because the Bureau might find itself getting radio information about hurricane Charlie from a military ship or plane whose code-name was also Charlie. So, mainly because young weathermen had for a long time referred to the storms on their charts by the names of their girl friends, the Bureau began giving them feminine names.

Now, to designate hurricanes on the Atlantic side of our continent, the Weather Bureau maintains four separate sets of girls' names in alphabetical order. It uses a different set each year and, when four years have gone by, starts again on the first list. Each year's earliest hurricane gets the A name. To date, no one year has brought enough storms to use the names far down the alphabet, like Vicky and Wilna. There are another four lists (with different names) for dubbing the hurricanes that occur on the Pacific side of the continent, off California and Mexico.

Pacific typhoons in the Far East are also known by girls' names, but for them a single list per year is not enough, because there are so many typhoons each year that they quickly exhaust the alphabet. So the weathermen have four alphabetical lists of typhoon names and, when one list is used up, they go on with the A name of the next. If one season's last storm is named Sally, the next year's opener will be called Tilda.

It is now the tradition that if a storm becomes very famous—for its death toll, its destructiveness, or its odd behavior—that storm's name is withdrawn from the lists for some years, so it does not risk being confused with a later storm of the same name. For example, the 1964 hurricanes Cleo, Dora, and Hilda, causing forty-six deaths and nearly half a billion dollars' worth of damages among them, were so destructive that their three names have been shelved, not to be used again for at least ten years. Hurricane Betsy of 1965, hurricane Beulah of 1967 and hurricane Camille of 1969 were even worse—so much worse that their names have been retired permanently from the lists.

Giving the storms ladies' names has not made them at all lady-like in their behavior. Hurricane Carol, in August of 1954, paralleled the course of 1938's notorious "New England hurricane" and nearly matched that one's destructiveness. Although Carol killed

# NAMES FOR ATLANTIC, CARIBBEAN, AND GULF OF MEXICO HURRICANES

## 1970

Alma    Becky    Celia    Dorothy    Ella    Felice    Greta
Hallie    Inez    Judith    Kendra    Lois    Marsha    Noreen
Orpha    Patty    Rena    Sherry    Thora    Vicky    Wilna

## 1971

Arlene    Beth    Chloë    Doris    Edith    Fern    Ginger
Heidi    Irene    Janice    Kristy    Laura    Margo    Nona
Orchid    Portia    Rachel    Sandra    Therese    Verna    Wallis

## 1972

Abby    Brenda    Candy    Dolly    Edna    Frances    Gladys
Hannah    Ingrid    Janet    Katy    Lila    Molly    Nita
Odette    Paula    Roxie    Stella    Trudy    Vesta    Wesley

## 1973

Anna    Blanche    Carol    Debbie    Eve    Francelia    Gerda
Holly    Inga    Jenny    Kara    Laurie    Martha    Netty
Orva    Peggy    Rhoda    Sadie    Tanya    Virgy    Wenda

# NAMES FOR PACIFIC HURRICANES (OFF MEXICO AND CALIFORNIA)

## 1970

Adele    Blanca    Connie    Dolores    Eileen    Francesca    Gretchen
Helga    Ione    Joyce    Kirsten    Lorraine    Maggie    Norma
Orlene    Patricia    Rosalie    Selma    Toni    Vivian    Winona

## 1971

Agatha    Bridget    Carlotta    Denise    Eleanor    Francene    Georgette
Hilary    Ilsa    Jewel    Katrina    Lily    Monica    Nanette
Olivia    Priscilla    Ramona    Sharon    Terry    Veronica    Winifred

1972

Annette   Bonny   Celeste   Diana   Estelle   Fernanda   Gwen
Hyacinth   Iva   Joanne   Kathleen   Liza   Madeline   Naomi
Orla   Pauline   Rebecca   Simone   Tara   Valerie   Willa

1973

Ava   Bernice   Claudia   Doreen   Emily   Florence   Glenda
Hazel   Irah   Jennifer   Katherine   Lilian   Mona   Natalie
Odessa   Prudence   Roslyn   Sylvia   Tillie   Victoria   Wallie

## NAMES FOR PACIFIC TYPHOONS
(used consecutively, regardless of year)

Agnes   Bess   Carmen   Della   Elaine   Faye   Gloria
Hester   Irma   Judy   Kit   Lola   Mamie   Nina
Ora   Phyllis   Rita   Susan   Tess   Viola   Winnie

Alice   Betty   Cora   Doris   Elsie   Flossie   Grace
Helen   Ida   June   Kathy   Lorna   Marie   Nancy
Olga   Pamela   Ruby   Sally   Tilda   Violet   Wilda

Anita   Billie   Clara   Dot   Ellen   Fran   Georgia
Hope   Iris   Joan   Kate   Louise   Marge   Nora
Opal   Patsy   Ruth   Sarah   Thelma   Vera   Wanda

Amy   Babe   Carla   Dinah   Emma   Freda   Gilda
Harriet   Ivy   Jean   Kim   Lucy   Mary   Nadine
Olive   Polly   Rose   Shirley   Trix   Virginia   Wendy

fewer people (sixty), it destroyed more than 460 million dollars' worth of property. Two months later, a hurricane named Hazel charged up through the midlands of North Carolina, Virginia, Maryland, and Pennsylvania, killing ninety-five people and doing damages of more than $250 million.

Nor did the newly named typhoons behave any better in their part of the world. In September of 1954, typhoon Marie rolled over Japan, killing 1,700 people, sinking 600 ships, and collapsing 20,-000 buildings.

In midsummer of 1955, hurricane Connie sloshed up the eastern seaboard of the United States, doing little damage but dumping between six and twelve inches of rain along its course. When Connie departed, rivers and ponds were at brink level, lakes were lapping over their banks, reservoirs were up to the tops of their dams. Then, in August, hurricane Diane arrived with another load of rain.

From Pennsylvania to Massachusetts, the river and lake banks overflowed, the dams collapsed. Wherever there was a channel—no matter what it had held before: a river, a creek, a brook—a flood poured down it. The waters tore away and carried along with them trees, farm buildings, the carcasses of cattle and deer. When the flood came to a town, it mashed up all this debris against the town's bridges. Thus damming itself, the water spread out sideways all through the town's streets. Soon the bridges gave way under the pressure and let loose the pent-up flood—more of it now, and more terrible—to boom on downstream to the next town.

Many of the cities of the northeast are mill towns, built close along a river's bank, their narrow streets crowded with factories. In some of these the water rose to forty feet above the highest flood level ever known before. Forty feet would be a monstrous tide for even an ocean to throw up. In these close-clustered cities it came like the end of the world (and for more than two hundred people it was). The water washed away whole blocks of houses in one gulp. Trains in railroad yards came uncoupled and their cars, like matchbox toys, bobbed away on the flood. In Putnam, Connecticut, the water broke into a magnesium plant and broke out again, laden with barrels of the dangerous metal. (Magnesium is what incendiary bombs are made of. An ordinary kitchen match will set it afire, but that fire is very hard to put out.) Somehow the floating barrels did explode into blue-white flame and, all night long, Putnam's horrified citizens watched a fire-topped flood seething about their town's streets.

Diane got the temporary title of "America's first billion-dollar hurricane." But after all the reports were in, its toll of damage turned out to be slightly less than a billion—$832,000,000. And Diane ought to share the blame with the earlier hurricane Connie, which made a good deal of the later destruction possible.

Ten years later, America did get its first billion-dollar hurricane, with the arrival of Betsy in September of 1965. This storm, which raked the Gulf shores of Florida, Alabama, Mississippi, and Louisiana, has rightly been called "the most devastating tropical storm ever to strike the American mainland." When the Government's hurricane experts went into Louisiana afterward to evaluate the damage there, those veterans of many another disaster could only describe what they found as "incredible."

Betsy's death toll was very small compared to that of several lesser storms, but its destruction of property amounted to $1,400,-000,000—nearly a billion and a half—almost five times the cost of the once-great New England hurricane. The dead numbered only 75, but 860 other people were hospitalized, while nearly 22,-000 were less seriously injured or became ill from exposure and shock. In the four states some 2,900 homes were totally destroyed; 24,000 homes suffered major damage, and another 120,000 homes endured less serious damage.

Besides the tempest of wind, torrents of rain, and tumult of storm waves, Betsy's victims had to contend with such additional bizarre miseries as a plague of snakes which emerged from the Louisiana bayous, crazed by the salt water that had flooded their usual haunts. In the Mississippi River at Baton Rouge, the storm

*If this aerial photograph had been taken a day earlier, it would have shown only the swirling storm wave of 1965's hurricane Betsy surging over this area of Louisiana near New Orleans. Now, after the wave's subsidence, boats are left perched high on docks or dry land, houses are smashed or toppled into the channel—and several are left straddling the highway.*

*AMERICAN RED CROSS*

sank a freight scow loaded with drums containing 600 tons of deadly chlorine. Even after the hurricane was over, the city's residents had to stand ready to run for their lives, while dredgers worked gingerly to raise the scow. If the drums had sprung a leak, that whole stretch of the river would have bubbled with escaping chlorine gas, and the city would have been blanketed with its killing vapor. Fortunately, that added peril was averted; the scow was raised and the drums salvaged without incident.

The most recent really outstanding hurricane was 1969's Camille. As it rumbled north through the Gulf of Mexico its central winds were estimated at 190 to 200 miles per hour, making it one of the most powerful hurricanes ever recorded, with the strongest winds to hit America since the Florida Keys' Labor Day hurricane of 1935. But Camille first touched the mainland—on the night of Sunday, August 17, 1969—at the nearly uninhabited tip of Louisiana. Sweeping across that marshland, its winds were blunted a bit; they were blowing at a slightly less lethal 150 m.p.h. by the time the hurricane reached populated areas.

Warnings of Camille's approach had allowed hundreds of thousands of Gulf Coast dwellers to flee to shelter farther inland, but the storm was a killer nevertheless. (When the police chief of Pass Christian, Mississippi, warned a houseful of people that the ocean was washing over the town's seawall, the people paid no attention. They were throwing "a hurricane party," they said, and were having too much fun to leave. "That," said the chief afterward, "was the last anybody saw of them.")

The towns that Camille hit head-on in Mississippi virtually vanished from existence. The storm wave, twenty-five feet high, thundered over Pass Christian like a steamroller. Of the community's three thousand houses—many of them grand mansions dating from before the Civil War—every one was either demolished or severely damaged. After the wave, said a survivor, the town resembled "a lumber yard." In a single apartment building, twenty-three people drowned.

Before the storm, the resort city of Biloxi had boasted scores of tremendous and elegant luxury motels; after Camille's passing, only two remained standing. At the seaport of Bay St. Louis, exactly half of the business district blew away. The harbor city of Gulfport was all but leveled of buildings, and giant ships were thrown ashore in their place.

The exact toll of Camille's victims may never be known, because many people died uncounted in the back-country swamplands of Mississippi and Louisiana. But an early tally of those killed in the communities along the coast reached 153. Hundreds more were missing, and tens of thousands were homeless. More than a score of vessels—from tugboats to 10,000-ton freighters—were sunk or dashed aground. Dozens of cargo trailer-trucks on the Gulf highways were flipped over and smashed.

The total of Camille's cost in damages hasn't yet been added up. The destruction of homes, cars, and other private property was expected to reach about half a billion dollars, and the damage to military and government installations around the Gulf was thought to be equally great. The storm may also have cost the local oil and fishing industries almost $200,000,000 in lost equipment and interrupted business.

Within a day after ravaging the Gulf Coast, Camille's hurricane spiral began to uncoil and weaken. The killing winds diminished, and the storm became just a vast squall of rain-spilling cloud that moved northeastward across the continent. But even in that less terrible form, Camille continued to spread devastation. In the one day of August 20, 1969, it poured ten inches of rain onto the rugged mountain country of western Virginia.

The downpour set loose avalanches which, said an observer, "stripped trees and earth down to the bare mountain granite." Swollen rivers boiled through the narrow valleys, the worst flood that Virginia had suffered in more than a century. The towns of Buena Vista, Glasgow, Scottsville, and dozens of smaller communities were all but washed away. At last count, 105 people had

*These people await rescue by their house which the 150-mile winds of hurricane Camille in 1969 left high and dry on the railroad tracks between Gulfport and New Orleans.*

*WIDE WORLD PHOTOS*

drowned or been buried by landslides, 57 others were still missing and, again, the full toll may never be known. An early estimate set property damage in the state at $113,000,000.

Unquestionably, Camille will turn out to have been another in the billion-dollar class of destroyers, and will probably rank after 1965's Betsy as America's second most costly storm to date. Camille's nearest competitor for that dubious honor would have been hurricane Beulah of 1967. That storm took only about one hundred lives, the majority of them in the Caribbean islands and Mexico, but most of its billion dollars' worth of property damage was done in Texas, where it crippled a number of fishing ports and then wiped out 70 percent of the state's valuable pepper and citrus fruit crops.

Beulah's example showed how a storm can blight its victims' lives or interfere with their livelihood in any number of ways besides killing them outright. A hurricane may spoil the fishing for some seaside community by smashing and sinking its fleet of fishing boats. But sometimes it destroys the fish instead. The massive tides and currents stirred up by a hurricane's storm wave can roil the depths of a sea so that deep-lying layers of water are lofted nearer the surface. The fish that lived in that water when it was at deep-sea pressures, and which now are lifted up along with it, cannot survive the suddenly lessened pressure. The fish literally explode. After hurricane Janet, in 1955, the natives of Swan Island in the Caribbean reported that their beaches were covered with dead fish, "almost all with their eyes popped out."

In other hurricanes and typhoons, when storm waves hurled the ocean far inland on coastal plains, the flood tides soon subsided but they often left great areas so impregnated with corrosive sea salt that nothing would grow there for years afterward. The storm's winds can also destroy extensive stands of forest. If a tree is so solidly rooted that a hurricane can't blow it over, the storm can still kill it by blowing at 125 miles an hour. A wind of that speed, freighted with pebbles, gravel, and abrasive sand, will peel the bark off a tree. The effect is much the same as a forest fire; a tree can die of such injuries, and often does. In some places—Cuba is one—forests of dead, clean, white, ghostly poles stand where trees used to.

A killer storm can take its toll in the sky, as well. Its winds slap many birds out of the air. Swifter birds, fleeing before the storm, will alight on what looks like sanctuary, only to have the hurricane catch up and sweep over them. On the island of Jamaica, after every storm the natives pick up thousands of sea birds that have been dashed to death against the trees in which they sought shelter.

At other times, whole flocks of birds may survive the storm long enough to get safely inside its calm eye. In that windless area they rest on their wings and wait for the rage around them to diminish. But the eye can carry them thousands of miles and eventually set them loose in an alien land and climate where they cannot live. Tropical birds like the man-o'-war have been seen in such unlikely places as New York City after the passing of a hurricane. Others have been carried to Hudson's Bay or Greenland, to perish from the cold.

Still, for all their calamity and caprice, there are a few hurricanes to be found among the storm records that are worthy of some commendation. In 1730, the once lush, green, and flowery island of Martinique was being gnawed bald by a plague of red ants, until a hurricane came along and drowned the ant population. It is worth noting that every island in the West Indies might never have been anything *but* bare, if it had not been for the hurricanes that blew over them in prehistoric days.

Those islands, and the shores of larger lands in all the tropic seas, have stands of coconut palms and mangrove trees which help to hold down the soil that supports everything else that grows. The coconuts and mangroves are there because their big, hard-shelled seeds can float for a long time in sea water without being harmed. Ages ago, the hurricane tore these seeds off their parent trees and washed them from island to island in the far-traveling storm waves. No botanist today can tell where the very first "ancestor" coconuts and mangroves grew, because the storms have spread their descend-

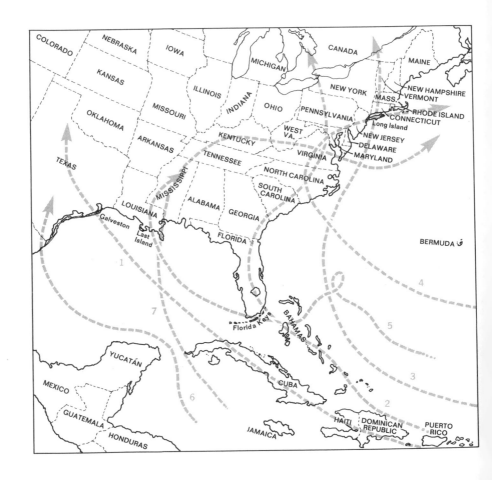

*Tracks of some of the more outstanding "bad" hurricanes described in this chapter: (1) the great Galveston storm of 1900; (2) the 1928 storm that drowned 1,836 people with the waters of Florida's Lake Okeechobee; (3) the New England hurricane of 1938; (4) the flood-bringing hurricane Diane of 1955; (5) hurricane Betsy of 1965, the most destructive storm ever to hit the United States; (6) hurricane Beulah of 1967; and (7) hurricane Camille of 1969.*

ants through the length and breadth of the tropical seas. Other plants that owe their far-flung sowing to the hurricane or typhoon are the sapote and the yellow mombin (both edible fruits and important items in the diet of tropical peoples), plus purely decorative trees like the casuarina and numerous different palms.

Even those two terrible "sister storms," Connie and Diane, did some good, though they rather overdid it. When they flooded the northeastern United States in the summer of 1955, they at least put an end to a severe drought that had been strangling the area for four long years. Before their coming, rain had been so scarce in the northeast that crops were dying, reservoirs were depleted down to damp mud, and New York City was on the verge of rationing drinking and bath water. The flood left enough water reserves that the locality didn't have to fear another shortage for ten years.

The killer storm is seldom either all bad or all good. Connie and Diane drowned people in the country while they were allaying the thirst of people in the city. The 1588 hurricane defeated the Invincible Armada, and the English thought that a very good deed, but the Spanish decidedly did not. The 1889 typhoon over Samoa prevented a war in the making, but it killed 150 sailors who might have preferred to take their chances in combat.

It is not likely that the hurricane and typhoon will ever shed their reputation of being out-and-out "killer" storms. To the contrary, their reputation is sure to get steadily worse, because every new storm that rages over the face of the planet finds more things and more people to pulverize. At the time this book is being written, hurricane Betsy holds the record as the world's most costly storm, and the Bay of Bengal typhoon still stands as the most murderous. But by the time you read these words, another storm may already have topped either record.

# 7
## THE KILLER'S
## KID SISTER

Anyone who has read *The Wonderful Wizard of Oz* knows what a tornado is: the sudden, circling, snatching storm that picked up Dorothy Gale and her little dog Toto from their bleak Kansas farm and set them down again, many hours and miles later, "in the midst of a country of marvelous beauty," the land of the Munchkins, on the outskirts of Oz.

Before he wrote that famous book, Frank Baum had been a newspaperman in the midwestern United States. It's probable that he got the idea for Dorothy's storm from one notable tornado that hit Irving, Kansas, in 1879. That storm first lifted a large iron bridge off the Blue River and wadded it up like a piece of tin foil, then went on to mash the town of Irving as flat as the corn fields around it. The few families in the area who lived through the devastation were so terrorized that for weeks afterward they never all went to bed at the same time, but kept someone awake and on watch in each house, to cry a warning if another storm should come.

That tornado got a great deal of publicity and was described in detail, as "the great Kansas cyclone," in newspapers all over the world. It seems likely that Frank Baum remembered the storm twenty years later when he wrote the *Wizard of Oz*. Certainly the rest of the world remembered. People still call the tornado a "Kansas cyclone" and still call Kansas "the cyclone state."

Neither name is quite accurate. The state of Iowa has more such storms, in proportion to its area, than Kansas does. And the storm is a "cyclone" only in a very general sense. A hurricane is also a cyclone, and so is almost any rainstorm, and so may be a gentle breeze. The word "cyclone," in weathermen's technical language, refers to any low pressure area of air with winds spiraling around and into it, and such a low may be as small as a backyard or as big as half a continent. It is unfortunate, because it's confusing, that the general word "cyclone" should be casually applied to such a distinctive kind of cyclone as the tornado. (The word is loosely used in India, too; the typhoons there are called cyclones, when really they're just one more *sort* of cyclone.) "Tornado" is a better, more specific name for the storm (it comes from the Spanish word for "turning") or the popular nickname "twister" is an apt description of the storm's behavior.

Tornadoes have occurred in every one of the continental United States, in every month of the year (though they're more frequent from March through September) and at every hour of the day and night. They have ravaged both empty countryside and crowded cities. In America the biggest metropolis ever to be hard-hit by a tornado is St. Louis, Missouri; but, abroad, both London and Moscow have been struck. Tornadoes probably have happened at some time in nearly every country in the world's temperate zones. They have been reported in Australia, China, France, Germany, Holland, Hungary, India, Italy, Japan, Mexico, and the islands of Bermuda and Fiji.

*The first bulge of a tornado starts to grope downward from its cloud cover toward the earth. A few moments later, it was a full-grown funnel extending from clouds to ground and starting its destructive march across country.*

*ESSA*

The main reason they have kept the name of "Kansas cyclones" is that, in all the world, their favorite haunt is the American midwest, where the great level plains seem to provide the ideal conditions for them. Ever since covered-wagon days, the midwesterners have been enduring one tornado after another. For a long time they didn't understand much about the twister except that it was a fearsome killer and destroyer. They knew that it smashed things and threw things and often threw them high into the air, all of which they attributed to its violent, whirling winds. But they could not figure out why or how it did some of the fantastic things that it did.

For one, the tornado smashed churches in preference to saloons. This was odd, but it was so. In town after town that a twister passed through, if it demolished just one building, that building was usually a church. If it leveled the whole town except for one building left standing, that building was usually a saloon.

This went on for years, all over the midwest, and nobody could explain it. The saloonkeeper, the town drunk, and other impious people made jokes about it, while devout and righteous people were puzzled and exasperated by the phenomenon. It did seem to them that if God or Fate or Mother Nature was going to visit destruction on the things men built, the havoc ought rightly to start with such iniquitous places as grog-shops and skip the houses of worship.

Finally someone figured out why. The explanation not only gave man some insight into the workings of the tornado, it also showed him how to protect his buildings against at least one hazard of the storm. Since that time, the twisters have knocked down a good many more buildings, and continue to do so, but the churches are no longer the likeliest victims, and the saloons are no longer the likeliest to be spared.

(The explanation is a simple one, and it will become apparent to you as you read on. But in the meantime, just for an exercise in puzzle-solving, you might like to try to reason it out for yourself. Why the damage to churches and not saloons?)

˄ The tornado develops from an area of warm, light air which, in rising, attracts cooler, heavier air into the area and imparts to it a spin that gradually becomes a highspeed whirlwind surrounding an upward-sucking interior draft—which sounds very like the description of a hurricane or typhoon. In these essentials, the tornado *is* akin to the bigger storms, which is why it's sometimes called their "kid sister."

To understand how the tornado differs from them, imagine that a hurricane is squeezed, to compress both its bulk and its energy. The 20-mile-wide eye becomes no bigger around than, say, a city block. The air that had been briskly rising through the eye's broad chimney will now be literally whistling up this constricted tube. The hurricane's vast banks of clouds are squeezed until they're just a thin, tight sheath around that narrow updraft. The winds that may have taken half an hour to blow all the way around the hurricane's perimeter will now take just a fraction of a second to whip around this slender pipe.

The resulting storm is the equivalent of a giant and powerful vacuum cleaner. It acts like one and it looks like one (the modern tank-type cleaner with a long hose ending in a nozzle and brush). The tight sheath of cloud, whirling so fast that it appears solid, forms the vacuum cleaner's hose. Its nozzle is on the ground and its "tank" is somewhere above the layer of clouds that covers the sky. As this dangling hose moves along, the snarling circle of wind around its nozzle acts like a cleaner's brush, scouring the ground clean of everything it touches, and the "sweepings" are sucked up by the voracious updraft inside the hose.

˅The classic shape of the tornado is that of a funnel, with its narrow end on the earth, broadening to where it joins the main body of clouds in the sky. But often it is shaped just like a hose, or a rope, the same diameter all the way up. Occasionally it may resemble an hour-glass, broad on the ground, thin-waisted in the middle, thick again above. Sometimes the tornado stands stiffly vertical as it moves. More often, because the winds aloft are hurrying its upper

*The dread black funnel of a tornado cloud churns into the city of Wichita Falls, Texas, in 1964. This twister shifted a ten-story office building off its foundations.*

AMERICAN RED CROSS

end along while the nozzle end drags more slowly across the ground, the hose portion is strung out at an angle to the earth. It often stretches and contracts, like a worm, and, wormlike, it may writhe and twist and even kink itself into momentary loops. Whatever its shape, the hose is always accompanied, at the nozzle end, by a cloud of dust that it's kicking up from the ground as it churns along. At least, the ground cloud looks like dust from a distance. In reality it may consist of boulders, trees, houses, trucks, mangled animals—everything smashable and grabbable that stood in the twister's way.

If there is something that a tornado can't knock down with the wind-wall around its funnel or gulp up with the suction inside, it often makes that thing destroy itself. The sucking inside the funnel is done by its column of incredibly low air pressure. When this envelopes any sort of hollow object, the instantaneous drop in pressure around that object is so extreme that its own normal interior air billows outward with a force of some 170 pounds per square inch. Result: explosion. (A hurricane's eye produces the same sort of effect, but the tornado's pressure-drop is incomparably greater and more sudden.) A house may blow itself to smithereens when a tornado funnel passes over it, or all the tires on an automobile may burst, or canned goods may explode their tins, or soda bottles may blow their tops.

This is the reason why for so many years churches went to pieces in tornadoes when saloons did not. The churches were open only for worship services, and shut-up during the rest of the week. The taverns were open for business all week long, day and night, and if they had doors at all these were just light, swinging panels. When a tornado funnel dropped over a saloon, a well ventilated building, the air pressure inside could quickly equalize with the suddenly lowered pressure outside, without having to blow off the roof or a wall to do it. Once people realized this fact, they learned to keep a door or window always open in their houses (and churches). The building might still be blown down, but it wouldn't blow itself up.

Beyond that, man has not learned a great deal else to help him cope with the twister. Its causes and mechanics are even more of a mystery than those of the hurricane. Although tornadoes often form within the sight of human observers, they don't do it slowly like the hurricane, so there is no hope of scrutinizing the stages from early build-up to murderous maturity.

One theory of the cause of tornadoes—those that afflict the midwestern United States, anyway—is that a wave of air comes oozing eastward over the top of the Rocky Mountains and in the middle of the great plains meets another wave coming north from the Gulf of Mexico. The first wave, having dropped all its moisture while climbing the mountains, is very cool and dry. The Gulf wave is warm and loaded with moisture. Normally, cool air meeting warm air simply slides underneath it. But this mountain air, since it's coming down from a great height, finds itself on top of the warm wave. That air, because it is warm, insists on rising but finds itself held down by the cool blanket.

*A photograph of an (comparatively rare) invisible tornado. The twister dangles from the cloud layer above, but the only evidence of it is the dust and other debris it kicks up as it crosses this midwestern field.*

*ESSA*

In this tense situation, only a portion here and there of the warm air manages to bulge its way upward, rather like an escaping bubble, and so goes up in a "pop" of considerable speed. Other air, rushing into the space it has vacated, is given the usual twist by the earth's rotation; and, because the area involved is so small, this air's spin is very tight and rapid.

Usually the turbulent action of air fighting air occurs in an already cloudy and stormy-looking sky, because the meeting of the cool and warm waves has condensed the latter's moisture into a heavy cloud cover. The spinning begins high among those clouds, but almost immediately starts to extend itself into a column. Since any upward growth is discouraged by the heavy layer of cool air above, the spiral extends itself downward through the warm and less dense air below. It becomes visible now, because it drags down shreds of the cloud it descends from, and also its own wind cools and condenses into cloud the moisture in the air it descends through. This is when the typical funnel- or hose-shaped cloud dangles from the sky and gropes its way to earth.

There may have been many of these disturbances along the junction where the mountain air and Gulf air met, so it is not at all unusual for several or dozens or even scores of tornadoes to develop simultaneously. Sometimes two separate funnels will brush and merge into one, or one will divide into two or more. Sometimes a funnel will charge along the earth for a while, then retract partway or all the way into its overhead cloud, perhaps skipping one house or a town, then snake down to the ground again and resume its course of destruction.

It might seem that weathermen, when they observe that waves of mountain air and Gulf air are about to overlap, could predict exactly when and where tornadoes will appear. But the best they can do is to warn that tornadoes are "likely," because often the colliding air masses work off their tension by producing mere thunderstorms, though they may be fierce ones. Since the overlap of air masses generally extends over several states, it is hard to say

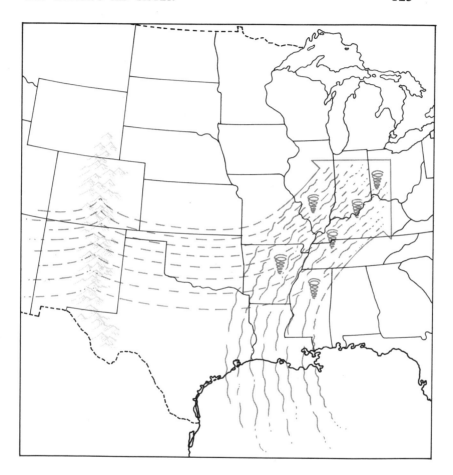

*Tornadoes usually travel to the northeast from their point of origin, follow-ing the "current" where mountain air and Gulf air merge and deflect north-ward.*

just where in that vast area warm air "bubbles" will succeed in bobbing up through the cool blanket, or when they'll do it, or whether that movement will provoke the spin of air that will start a twister.

All the conditions that are required to trigger a tornado are not known. Although a weatherman may suspect that a particular piece of sky contains all the necessary ingredients for a twister, he cannot be sure until he sees the funnel actually writhing before him. But by then, so quickly does the tornado burst into full growth, it's too late to identify and analyze all the myriad weather elements that prevailed in the instant before. And as soon as a twister appears, it is such a dangerous and terrifying thing that nobody near it, not even a professional weatherman, can regard it with cool scientific detachment.

Almost all that is known about the tornado has been learned by observing it from a distance and by examining the traces it leaves behind. It generally travels to the northeast from its point of origin, following more or less the "current" where the mountain wave of air (moving east) and the Gulf wave (moving north) merge and deflect each other's direction so that their joint drift is northeastward.

A tornado's forward speed is usually about forty-five miles per hour, though some have dawdled as slowly as five miles an hour and others have clipped along at seventy. Occasionally the funnel will stop and stand practically still, chewing like a drill into the ground beneath it, then will move on, and may continue this stop-and-go progress throughout its career.

The average diameter of a tornado's "nozzle," hence the width of its path of destruction, is about 400 yards. But some have measured just thirty feet, and at least one ravening giant's track was two miles across. The typical tornado will travel ten to forty miles—the average is sixteen—between its birthplace and its point of disappearance. Yet one twister set a record distance of 293 miles. It is impossible to predict how long any particular tornado will last. The twister, like the hurricane, dies when its energy supply of heat and moisture (or either one of these) falters in the support of its circulation system.

The tornado usually coils down from an ominously ugly sky on a hot and sticky day. It may be preceded by rain or hail, and is generally followed by a heavy downpour. The tornado can appear from any kind of cloud, but the one cloud formation that almost always warns of "twister coming!" is the mammatoform—clouds shaped like women's breasts, greenish-black, they bulge downward, and there are hundreds of them hanging from the sky.

*These are the eerie mammatoform, or breast-shaped, clouds—dangling greenish-black pouches that are an almost sure sign of tornadoes.*

*ESSA*

Sometimes, though, when the mountain and Gulf waves of air first overlap, the tornado-triggering turbulence can start even before any clouds form; so it is possible that a twister can develop in what had been, just moments before, a clear sky. In such a case, where none of the air involved has yet had any of its moisture condensed into clouds, the tornado itself may be invisible.

The twister comes with a noise so frightful that it gives adequate warning of a killer on the march. Various survivors' ear-witness accounts have described the noise in different ways. "Like the howl of dozens of sirens." "Like a giant blowtorch." "Like the roar of hundreds of airplanes." "Like that of a thousand cannons." For a long time it was believed that the noise was caused by the tornado's wild winds. Undoubtedly they contribute to it, but now it is fairly certain that the noise is that of thunder inside the funnel.

The energy engine of a tornado can build up electrical charges far greater than any thunderstorm's, so the twister often arrives with a spectacular display of lightning outside and around it, sometimes in striking colors: yellow, green, blue, purple. The people who have seen the inside of a tornado's funnel—those few who have been in a position to look straight up the funnel as it skipped over them, and were lucky enough to live to tell about it— say there is even more lightning inside than outside. The survivors say the whole interior is lit up by lightning bolts, so extensive and so constant that they look like luminous lace draped around the inside of the swirling walls. Since each discharge of lightning causes a clap of thunder, and since the discharges inside the funnel are innumerable, simultaneous, and continuous, the tornado's characteristic noise is that of thunder endlessly booming.

The things that are not known about the tornado are guessed at; for example, the speed at which that infernal funnel spins. Just as there is yet no accurate way of clocking a hurricane's fastest winds, so the infinitely faster ones of a tornado cannot be measured. In 1953, after a twister tore down power-line towers in Massachusetts, the engineers who had designed the towers and knew what stresses they were built to withstand were able to estimate that the destroying winds must have been blowing at least 335 miles per hour. Other such evidence has led weathermen to believe that the funnel's wind-wall can spin as fast as 500 miles per hour.

In the same way, since the weight of some of the objects which tornadoes have lifted is known—including a railroad locomotive— it can be calculated that the air pressure inside that funnel must be about one third of sea-level normal, and the sucking winds inside it must be rocketing skyward at between one and two hundred miles per hour. There is no knowing how high that rushing column ascends—since all that can be seen of the "vacuum cleaner hose" is what hangs beneath the cloud cover—but there is reason to believe that it rises as high as 15,000 feet.

It is entirely possible that a tornado could knock over an object —say a cow—with a 500-m.p.h. wind that would hit it like a viciously swung hammer weighing twelve tons; then envelope it in a near-vacuum that would make every organ in the cow's body explode; then, with the suction of its nearly 200-m.p.h. updraft, suck up what's left (hamburger, by now) and in less than one minute whisk it three miles above the earth.

A tornado at some time has probably done just that; enough of them have done ghastlier thinks. A twister that hit a mill town in France, in 1845, smashed through a textile factory, picked up workmen and their metal looms together, and churned them about in mid-air until the machines minced the men to pieces.

The "tri-state tornado" of March 18, 1925, started in Missouri, crossed Illinois, and finally died in Indiana after killing 689 people, injuring 1,980 others, and causing property damage of more than sixteen and a half million dollars. One of the fastest traveling twisters ever recorded—making speeds of from 57 to 68 miles per hour—it covered 219 miles in less than four hours, leaving a trail of destruction from half a mile to a mile wide. Four towns

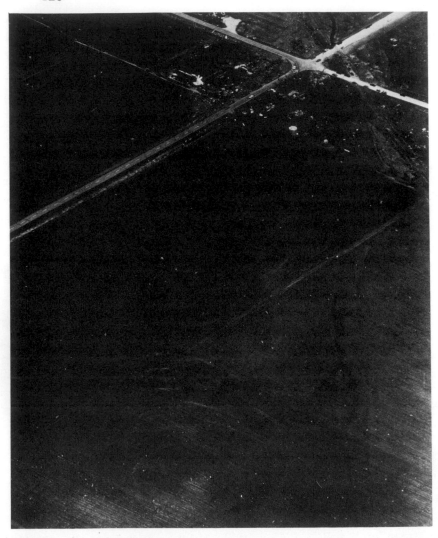

*A tornado in May, 1968, left the wreckage of a small Iowa community scattered about the crossroads at the top of the photograph, then scrawled its "signature" on the adjacent cornfields. Extending into the foreground of the photograph can be seen the spiraling scar carved by the funnel's scouring winds as it swirled off across the fields.*

ESSA

were practically smeared into the earth—Gorham, De Soto, and Parrish in Illinois and Griffin in Indiana. At Griffin not a single building was left standing. At Parrish only three of the town's five hundred inhabitants were left uninjured. The tri-state tornado still holds the black record of being the most murderous and destructive single twister ever to strike anywhere in the world.

In February, 1959, a middle-of-the-night tornado lashed at St. Louis, Missouri, the biggest city on the Mississippi River. The twister lasted just five minutes, but in that time it went through a heavily-populated area thirty blocks square, killing twenty-one people, seriously injuring eighty-three, destroying sixteen homes and thirty-one other buildings, damaging nearly two thousand others and leaving more than three thousand families homeless.

In the early evening of April 11, 1965, a family had just sat down to watch television in their home on an outlying street of Bluffon, Indiana, when they heard what sounded like a train pulling in to the Bluffon depot. The wife turned to her husband, puzzled, and said, "You can't hear trains out here. . . ." In that instant they realized what was upon them, seized up their children and ducked into their basement shelter. But it wasn't quite strong enough; while the mother and children survived unscathed, the father was badly injured. Their home and all their belongings were totally destroyed.

That family was not unique, but it was luckier than most. Later that same night, 155 miles away in Pittsfield, Ohio, a Red Cross rescue worker noted that "the only evidence that a community had existed here was a torn and twisted sign. All that was left were naked tree trunks, twisted metal, and scattered debris. . . ."

These are just two isolated reports of the devastation done on Palm Sunday, April 11, 1965. During that one day and night, a total of thirty-seven separate tornadoes touched down in five midwestern states—Illinois, Indiana, Michigan, Ohio, and Wisconsin—to kill 266 people, injure 3,261 more, destroy nearly 8,000 homes and more than 2,600 other buildings.

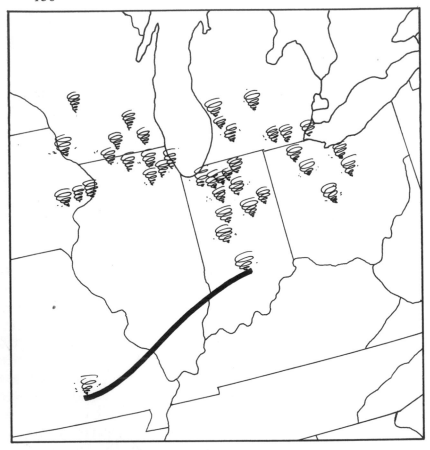

*The individual funnels show where the thirty-seven tornadoes touched down in six midwestern states on Palm Sunday, 1965. The lower track shows the 219-mile course of the "tri-state" tornado of 1925, the most murderous twister on record.*

The tornado has no scruples about striking twice in the same spot; its record of coincidences is higher than that of the hurricane. Oklahoma City has been hit 26 times since 1892. Austin, Texas, suffered two tornadoes in the same day of May 4, 1922. Baldwyn, Mississippi, was struck twice within twenty-five minutes on March 16, 1942. The town of Codell, Kansas, was assaulted every year for three straight years—1916, 1917, and 1918—on the same day, May 20. (The next May 20, in 1919, everybody in Codell was living underground, but no twister arrived that year, and none has hit the town since.)

It is not difficult to understand how the tornado can deal the death and destruction that it does. Its forces are greater in degree than the hurricane's, though less in extent. However, those forces can often interact mysteriously, to produce effects that are beyond explanation, and would be beyond belief, if they hadn't been proven by evidence and eye-witness testimony. Some of the effects have been violent, some almost absurdly gentle, some downright funny—all of them weird. At one time or another, a tornado has:

Impaled fragile, brittle straws deep in tree trunks and fence posts, as if they had been sharp and sturdy spears.

Blown a lighted kerosene lamp for a third of a mile, setting it down upright, unbroken, and still alight.

Sheared the wool off a whole herd of sheep, but left the denuded sheep grazing unperturbed and unharmed.

Scooped up a prairie pond, carried it for miles, and dumped onto a bewildered town its contents of several hundred frogs.

Picked up a 700-pound refrigerator and carried it for three miles before dropping it.

Pelted a farmer with sand and grit, as if by a shotgun, so that he wore the tattoo of it imbedded in his skin all the rest of his life.

Carried a whole herd of steers flying through the air over Kansas, where they looked, said an observer, "like a flight of gigantic birds."

A tornado that hit Topeka, Kansas, in 1966, shoved a ten-storey office building off its foundations. At Van Meter, Iowa, a twister popped a full-grown rooster inside a narrow necked two-gallon jug, alive and without a feather ruffled. At Harleyville, Kansas, a tornado passed close to a farmhouse and reached out to tweak the bedclothes and mattress from under one of the farm boys, leaving him unharmed and still sound asleep.

When a twister hit Greentown, Indiana, in 1965, Mr. and Mrs. Ray Hardin and their six-year-old daughter were caught at home with no chance to seek any better shelter than their hall closet. They huddled inside it while the tornado tore their house to flinders. When the storm cleared, the only thing still standing in the rubble was the closet containing the unharmed Hardins.

A Kansas farmer named Evans, who'd heard nothing of an approaching tornado until his house roof suddenly blew off, looked up to see his massive cast-iron kitchen stove "going round and round" right over his head. In another room, his 17-year-old daughter had all her clothes snatched off, but was otherwise unhurt.

As an example of the tornado's formidable strength, in 1931 one of them caught the Great Northern Railway's crack express train, *The Empire Builder,* while it was crossing Minnesota at sixty miles an hour. The twister toppled five of the train's 70-ton coaches off the tracks, picked up one of the coaches—carrying 117 passengers—and hurled it into a ditch eighty feet from the railroad. One passenger was killed and 57 were injured.

Six years later, in 1937, another tornado picked up a Rock Island steam locomotive from its tracks in a freight yard and set it down again, neatly, on an adjoining pair of tracks.

Railroad trains are not the only big vehicles that suffer from twisters. In November, 1968, a tornado danced about a Florida airport, picked up a heavy twin-engine DC-3 transport plane and dropped it precisely on top of a light sport plane, squashing it flat.

Only storybook characters get wafted to Oz, but some real people have been carried by tornadoes on journeys almost as un-believable as Dorothy's. At Ponca City, Oklahoma, an elderly man and wife were in their living room when their house suddenly jolted into the air. They were thrown to the floor and lay there watching the house disintegrate around them as it spun aloft. Everything fell apart except the floor on which they lay. Like a magic carpet, it gradually, gently glided back to earth and set down the old couple without a scratch.

In 1955, at Bowdle, South Dakota, a mother watched from a window while her nine-year-old daughter rode her pony in a field next to the house. Suddenly the pony, with the little girl still astride, shot high into the air. The mother dashed outdoors, but soon lost sight of the pair, as they were blown fully half a mile away. But the child was still in the saddle when the pony was set down; she suffered only a couple of minor bruises and the pony was not hurt at all.

If the tornado is the little sister of the hurricane, then the family has a couple of cousins in the two other weather phenomena known as the dust devil and the waterspout.

The dust devil—or sand devil or prairie whirlwind, as it is also called—is often seen pirouetting across a stretch of desert or a dry field or even an empty city lot. It looks something like a tornado:

*This air view of Wichita Falls, Texas, after the passing of the 1964 tornado, shows how the twister left its track of devastation through the city's suburbs.*
*AMERICAN RED CROSS*

a twirling pillar of dust, possibly carrying a litter of dead leaves and small twigs; but it's almost transparent and it is seldom tall enough to reach anywhere near the clouds.

Like the grander members of its family, the dust devil is a miniature energy engine. When a patch of ground gets hot, the air above it is warmed and rises, cooler air currents come spiraling in to replace it, and the process continues until the whirlwind cools the ground enough to interrupt the cycle. The hotter the ground, the longer and stronger the life of the dust devil, which is why they're taller and stouter over desert areas. As a general rule, a dust devil will last for as many hours as it is thousands of feet tall, but it is not common to see a very tall or long-lived dust devil outside of a desert like the Sahara. One was reported there, near Cairo, Egypt, that stood a mile high and lasted for five and a half hours.

There's not much danger connected with the dust devil. A railroad engineer once said he had felt his train shake as a Kansas dust devil hit it, but no real damage has ever been blamed on these prairie whirlwinds. They can never develop into a real tornado, because a tornado needs plenty of heat and moisture to fuel it. A dust devil may have the necessary heat, but it never has the moisture.

A closer cousin to the tornado is the waterspout. It *is* a tornado, in fact, which drops its funnel down onto a body of water instead of land. But this happenstance makes it nearly as harmless as the dust devil. The waterspout finds itself with too much moisture and not enough heat, because it sucks up such a spray of water that it soon cools its whole funnel to the point of breaking the energy cycle.

Adventure stories about the sea sometimes tell of a waterspout swamping a ship or bowling it over or even crashing right through it. These are exaggerations. A waterspout might conceivably flood and sink a small motorboat or blow over a small sailboat, but for anything larger it would have little more impact than a surge of spray coming in over the gunwale. A waterspout looks more fearsome than it is. That solid-seeming shaft is merely a tower of mist, and the weight of the mist slows down both the normally-vicious spiraling winds and the spout's forward speed. The adventure stories sometimes claim that the waterspout carries a sucked-up pillar of solid water, which it wields like a truncheon. A really big waterspout does heap up a mound of water inside its funnel, but this is never more than about eight feet high, and its traveling pace is so slow that it doesn't hit harder than an ordinary seashore breaker.

Like a terrestrial tornado, the waterspout can develop at night; when one does so over a subtropical sea, the mist that sheathes its funnel may teem with those microscopic sea organisms which glow when they're agitated (the same creatures that make a ship's bow wave phosphorescent). When that happens, the entire waterspout glows with a pale, pure white light and strides across the waters like the world's tallest ghost.

Since the tornado and the waterspout are essentially the same, if a twister forms over a terrain dotted with lakes, or if a waterspout forms over a sea speckled with islands, the one kind of storm can turn into the other. And one tornado in Utah once turned into what might be called a "snowspout." It formed over open, hot, flat country, but then climbed a still-snowcapped mountain. When the twister sucked up a field of snow it turned dead white for a while, then quickly cooled to the point of collapse.

Another tornado once developed over the coastal plains of Virginia, then briefly became a waterspout as it crossed a small river. (In crossing, it sucked the stream dry; after the twister passed, the riverbed was visible for some time, until it refilled again with flowing water.) The storm, now an ordinary tornado again, moved on to a harbor town on Chesapeake Bay. When it touched the Bay it became a waterspout once more and tossed some boats about. It reverted to a twister yet again as it came to a dock area, and there overturned a number of freight boxcars on a rail siding. It slid onto the water one more time, became a waterspout yet again, and then glided off across the Bay and out of sight of its astounded human audience on the shore.

# 8
# THE STORM WATCHERS

Twenty-three centuries ago, the Greek philosopher Aristotle wrote his *Meteorologia,* meaning "discourse on the atmosphere," which gave us our modern word "meteorology" for the science that studies weather and climate. In that book, Aristotle suggested that the worst storms are caused "when some winds are blowing and other winds fall on them." His fellow scientists of the day were equally sincere in their belief that thunder is caused by the clouds' bumping together. Today it is known that such ideas are naïve and preposterous, but it has not been known for very long.

For two thousand years after Aristotle, those simple notions might as well have been true and valid, because nobody could prove any different. During all that time, man had no scientific tools except the wind vane (or weathercock) to tell which way the wind was blowing, the rain gauge (a bucket set outdoors) to tell how much rain fell, and his own senses to perceive that the weather was hot, cold, ugly, muggy, or whatever. With what he had, though, he learned to do a passable job of weather prediction. Especially those people who lived outdoors and were most dependent on the weather

—farmers, fishermen, sailors—learned to read the clouds and winds for weather omens.

Less obvious signs, too, gave an observant man a fair idea of what kind of weather was headed his way. For example, he realized that the weather was going to change for the worse if the birds flew low, in short hops, and twittered a lot; if his horses became fidgety and his dogs quarrelsome; if he himself felt stiff and his joints ached. The man didn't know why these subtle signals presented themselves, but he knew that they meant stormy weather in the offing.

There is nothing magical or mysterious about these things. A storm comes with an area of low pressure air. When that begins to invade a locality, the birds notice it first; there's less buoyancy for their wings; they limit their flights and fuss noisily about the situation. The lower air pressure also allows gases and odors imprisoned in the soil to seep free; this bothers animals like horses and dogs that are sensitive to smells. Finally, an old man whose knees and elbows are already rheumatic—that is, creaky from the pressure of fluids accumulated in the bone sockets—will find that the lowered air pressure causes the fluids to expand inside those joints, and he feels the change as a dull ache.

It wasn't until a little over three centuries ago that more sophisticated instruments were developed to measure and analyze the weather. Men had long recognized that most liquids noticeably expand when they are warm and shrink when they are cold. Not until the close of the sixteenth century did one man, Galileo Galilei, think to put a colored liquid into a slender glass tube etched with degree marks, and so invent the thermometer to provide a standardized measurement of the air's temperature.

Evangelista Torricelli, fifty years later, in 1643, proved that air had weight. He took a long glass tube closed at one end, filled it with mercury, and stood it with the open end down in a wide dish also filled with the fluid metal. The mercury didn't pour out of the inverted tube; the surrounding air pressed down on the mercury in the dish heavily enough to hold a column of mercury upright inside the tube. Torricelli discovered that the column stood almost exactly thirty inches high when he did the trick in his laboratory (in a town near sea level), but that the column settled lower when he carried the contraption up a mountain.

The experiment showed that air weighs more at sea level where it's densely "packed" than it does at mountain height where there is less air above it pressing it down. It also became evident that, at any altitude, the mercury column was never permanently steady. It rose and fell by fractions of an inch, indicating local changes in air pressure. It always fell fastest and farthest, announcing a significantly low pressure, before and during storms. Torricelli had invented the barometer, then and now the one most necessary device for analyzing (and predicting) the weather.

At nearly the same time, in 1667, Robert Hooke invented a crude anemometer, a kind of windmill connected by a train of gears to a dial and pointer so that it measured how fast the wind was blowing. Someone anonymous discovered that a human hair absorbs moisture from damp air and thus stretches longer than when the air is dry. So he contrived the first hygrometer, in which the hair's slight stretching and contracting also moved a pointer, measuring the moisture content (or humidity) of the air around it.

These four instruments—the thermometer, barometer, anemometer, and hygrometer—have been often improved and made more sensitive since they first came into use in the 1600's. To this day they, plus the even older wind vane and rain gauge are the most important tools for the weatherman. But they never could, and still can't, indicate any conditions except those in their immediate vicinity. Until the 1800's, then, a meteorologist could not measure or analyze any weather other than what was going on in his area. This inability gave him a nearsighted view of the weather picture as a whole.

For example, as late as the mid-1700's, it was thought that a storm occurred in just one spot, although that spot might be hundreds of miles wide. The belief was that a storm stood still while it built up, blew its worst, and then died away, having spent its whole brief life over one area.

Daniel Defoe, the author of *Robinson Crusoe,* may have been the first man to suspect that a storm's life is not necessarily brief, and that it moves from place to place while it lives. In his account of a 1703 hurricane that battered England, he remarked that the storm "had been felt earlier" in the Americas. Defoe's observation was confirmed by Benjamin Franklin forty years later. Franklin was about to sail from Philadelphia to Boston when his ship was held in port by a furious thunderstorm. The storm was bad enough that Franklin figured it was a broad one, too, and must be lashing Boston at the same time. However, when he did reach Boston he learned that the weather there had been clear on the night Philadelphia was swamped, but that Boston had had a bad storm on the night following. Franklin guessed that the one storm had "surged from south to north," and became convinced that other storms must likewise travel.

About 1805, Sir Francis Beaufort, an admiral of the British Navy, set down what he knew about winds in the form of a scale on which they were ranked by their speeds, and a modified version of his scale is still used by weathermen today. Sir Francis classified the winds from Force 0 (dead calm) to Force 12 (hurricane) in a way that a sailor would best understand, according to the amount of sail that a ship of that era should or could carry in each kind of blow. In a Force 6 strong breeze of nineteen to twenty-four miles per hour "she could just carry in chase, full and by, royals and top-gallant sails," said the admiral. Today's Beaufort scale is less picturesque: a Force 6 breeze "makes telephone wires whistle."

It might seem that the scale is inadequate in providing no category beyond Force 12 (75 m.p.h. and up), since hurricane winds can go *so* much higher. However, the Beaufort Scale is mainly used in warning ships of a coming blow, and any captain who hears of a Force 12 wind in his area is going to head for safer waters. He could do no more if the wind were rated at Force 99.

In 1821, an American named William Redfield made a significant contribution to the understanding of the killer storms. Traveling through New England shortly after a hurricane had trampled the area, Redfield noticed that the trees blown down along the coast lay with their tops pointing toward the northwest, while those blown down inland pointed southeast. Redfield realized that this could only mean that the storm had consisted of a rotary wind blowing around a center that was itself moving forward.

A few years later the telegraph was invented, and man had his first means of almost instant communication. He found many uses for it, but from its earliest introduction in the 1840's he recognized its value in weather study and prediction. In 1743, Benjamin Franklin had had to go all the way to Boston, and spend a week doing it, to learn that his Philadelphia storm had not happened everywhere simultaneously. A hundred years later, with the telegraph, a meteorologist could check on the weather in any number of places and learn about it while it was happening.

By gathering reports from numbers of widely scattered observers, the meteorologists began to get an overall idea of the weather's behavior. They began to see that it resulted from a complicated interaction of conditions that might be far-flung and seemingly unrelated. They began to realize how weather moves from place to place, and how a cloudy sky over Chicago yesterday might mean a cloudburst over New York tomorrow.

Another use for the telegraph soon became apparent. In 1854, the French and English fighting against the Russians in the Crimean War suffered their worst naval "defeat" when a violent windstorm devastated their combined fleet of warships in the Black Sea. The French Minister of War sent an astronomer-meteorologist to investigate the disaster, to see if there might be some way of averting a repetition of it. Indeed there was, reported the scientist. That storm had not just blown up suddenly in the Black Sea; it had crossed most of Europe before descending on the fleet. If anyone had taken notice of its course and had taken the trouble to telegraph a warning ahead of it, the fleet could have been moved out of the storm's path. From that time on, the telegraph served the additional purpose of a storm alarm.

It was best put to use in the West Indies, by a volunteer weatherman known as "the hurricane priest." He was Father Benito Viñes, who set up a small meteorological laboratory in Havana, Cuba, in 1870. For twenty-three years he studied the killer storms, learned more about them than any other man of his time, wrote books to teach others about them and, most important of all, gave warning of their approach to every endangered community from the outermost Windward Islands to the coast of the United States.

In the beginning, Father Benito's laboratory consisted of a few cheap instruments contributed by his religious order, the Society of Jesuits, and he had only a pittance of money to work with. The priest devoted all of his time to this project, and succeeded in enlisting the unpaid services of many other people. He kept charts of every hurricane that passed, and all those that he could trace from years before. He visited the places they ravaged, questioned the survivors, and studied the damage. He was the first to make public what the original natives had known about the killer storms; for instance, that the rooster-tail clouds were an early warning signal.

Father Benito had willing assistants all over Cuba and the other islands to notify him (by collect telegram) whenever they spotted signs of a hurricane blowing up. When a ship's master had a brush with a storm at sea, he telegraphed Father Benito the news of its size and location as soon as he landed in port. From the scattered reports the priest would plot the storm's probable future course and, in turn, telegraph a warning to every sizeable town in its path. From each of these towns, the priest's volunteer helpers would gallop on horseback to warn other villages which had no telegraph.

Father Benito's largest expense was the transmission of the telegrams, though the Cuban telegraph and cable companies charged him only half the regular rate. But so valuable were his hurricane warnings that, after a while, other volunteers stepped in to pay the bill. They were the steamship companies, merchants' associations, insurance companies and Chambers of Commerce in cities as far away as the United States, who were grateful for his service. They not only paid his telegraph bills, they installed direct lines of their own to his monastery office, and contributed funds to buy more and better equipment for his laboratory.

Even the best laboratory in those days was rather primitive, and hurricanes were just as frustratingly capricious then as now, so Father Benito's predictions were not infallibly accurate. But, for a one-man weather bureau, he did a praiseworthy job and certainly saved countless lives. One reason the Americans on the mainland were so appreciative of his efforts was that they didn't have much of a weather bureau at all.

The United States Weather Service had been officially organized in 1870. It was first set up as a service of the U.S. Army's Signal Corps, which in a way was sensible, because the Signal Corps at that time operated most of the telegraph equipment in America. However, the Army was inclined to think of its new Weather Service people as soldiers first and meteorologists second. It made them waste a lot of time in learning to march, fencing with sabers, and practicing to defend their weather shacks against attack.

Soon after it was set up, the Weather Service stationed observers in the West Indies to keep a hurricane lookout, and to cable weather reports to a central office in Washington, D.C., which would issue storm warnings when necessary. However, practically everybody in the hurricane zone found Father Benito's forecasts much more expert and reliable, and continued to support his one-man enterprise. The Weather Service outposts closed down after only three years of operation.

By 1891, most of the telegraph systems in the United States were being run by private companies, so there was no longer any reason for the Weather Service to be a Signal Corps outfit. It was renamed the Weather Bureau and transferred to the U.S. Department of Agriculture. For the next few years it devoted most of its attention to serving farmers, by issuing bulletins on the most favorable planting seasons, harvesting seasons, etc.

Three new circumstances soon brought the Weather Bureau back into the storm-watching business. For one, Father Benito Viñes died in 1893. Although his work was continued by other Cuban volunteers, many American citizens and companies in the West Indies thought a U.S. government agency should take up the priest's work. Then, in 1896, a hurricane that Father Benito's successors had missed hit the United States without warning and killed 114 people on its way from Florida through Pennsylvania. The third circumstance was that a war was brewing between the United States and Spain, bound to blaze up at any time. Since Cuba was a Spanish colony, part of the war would have to be fought in those waters. Since Cuba would undoubtedly silence its storm-warning system, the effect would be that the United States would be fighting unannounced hurricanes at the same time. Under these several pressures, the Weather Bureau again set up its storm-watch stations, not among the islands this time, where they could be cut off by the war, but around the Gulf of Mexico.

As it turned out, when the war did commence in 1898, Cuba did not silence its hurricane warning system. The Spanish Government allowed the Cuban weather stations to go on telegraphing storm reports which any friend or enemy with a receiving set could listen to. It is said that the United States took unsporting advantage of this. If the story is true, an American spy in Havana managed to insert into one of Cuba's weather reports a coded message revealing that the Spanish Navy's entire Atlantic Fleet was lurking in the Cuban harbor of Santiago. Whether the spy story is true or not, the U.S. Navy did trap the Spanish fleet there, and destroyed it. That was one of the decisive actions which defeated Spain and broke its empire. The war ended with Cuba given into the United States' protection.

With the Gulf coast observation stations it had set up just before the war and the long-experienced stations it had acquired in its new protectorate of Cuba, the United States now had an extensive hurricane-warning system, which it continued to extend and improve. One improvement at this time was the invention of wireless telegraphy. Now ships could carry a telegraph set on board, and flash the news of storms while they were still far out at sea. Also, if a ship was headed toward a known storm, an on-shore station could warn it away from the danger.

But this didn't always work out to everyone's advantage. When a hurricane hit Key West, Florida, in 1919, the weather station there immediately flashed a warning which cleared every ship out of the open seas of the Gulf of Mexico. Then the weather station lost track of the hurricane, as it darted off at an unexpected angle. It was *somewhere* in the Gulf, but now there were no ships in the area to report on its whereabouts. The result was that the storm sneaked across the Gulf to the Texas coast and smashed into the city of Corpus Christi, doing an exceptional amount of damage and killing because the city had not been warned to prepare for it.

This problem continued to frustrate the meteorologists for twenty more years, as wireless telegraphy gave way to the even better and faster communication provided by voice radio. More and more ships were equipped with radios and, in theory, should have provided the shore stations with plenty of information for tracking hurricanes all the way in from their breeding grounds. In actuality, though, whenever one vessel reported stumbling onto a storm, every other ship in the area heard the message and shied away to safer waters, leaving the weathermen in the dark from then on. The only vessels that would deliberately loiter in the vicinity of a hurricane were Navy and Coast Guard ships doing it under orders.

However, the comparatively few and hasty reports from mid-ocean were more than had been available before, and the meteorologists gradually accumulated a great deal of new knowledge about the killer storms. From the ship-sightings, the meteorologists learned that the early-season storms usually form in the Caribbean Sea or the Gulf of Mexico. By July, the storms are being born farther to the east, outside the Caribbean in the Atlantic. Through August, the storms come from farther and farther east. During the peak season—the last week of August and the first week of September—the storms are born on the other side of the Atlantic, in the Cape Verde Islands, and those storms are almost always the worst. After September, the "hurricane cradle" moves westward once more, until the late-season storms are breeding again in the Caribbean and Gulf area.

The more the meteorologists learned about the killer storm, the more they realized they didn't know. As late as the 1940's, all the hurricane reports they received were from ground or sea level. By now they had developed the technique of sending weather instruments high into the atmosphere by balloon on fairly calm days, and they realized that upper-air conditions were often a more important factor in weather-making than any conditions that could be observed from the earth's surface. They desperately needed to know more about what went on in the upper levels of a hurricane, but obviously balloons would be of no use in that turmoil of winds.

The ideal vehicle for such research was the airplane. But airplanes did not yet have the range to seek out baby hurricanes in their breeding grounds. And by the time a hurricane got within reach of an airplane it was full-grown and full of fury. What airplane could survive an encounter with it? What pilot would dare to get anywhere near it?

Pilot Joseph P. Duckworth would.

In 1943, the middle of World War II, he was a major in the U.S. Army Air Corps, training other military pilots at a Texas airbase. On the afternoon of July 27, Major Duckworth and a navigator, Lieutenant Ralph O'Hair, were aloft in a light, single-engine AT-6 training plane at the same time that a hurricane was approaching the Texas coast near Galveston. Major Duckworth flew over there for a look at the storm from a respectful distance. Then he flew the fragile plane right into the swirling black wall of clouds, through the staggering blasts of wind and into the storm's eye. He circled for a while in that calm air, then plunged through the cloud wall again into the clear sky beyond, and headed back to his base.

The weather officer there, Lieutenant William Jones-Burdick, heard Duckworth's account of his flight. He found the story so nearly unbelievable that he insisted the pilot go up again, and take him along. With Jones-Burdick aboard, Duckworth calmly repeated his previous flight into, through, and out of the storm. The first man ever to fly deliberately into a hurricane had done it twice in one afternoon.

Now that it was proved that a comparatively flimsy airplane could go where the stoutest ship often could not—because the plane did not buck the winds but rode with them—the airplane quickly became the farthest-seeing eyes of the storm watchers. By the following May of 1944, the Air Corps had assigned a unit of the Air Weather Service to the sole duty of tracking the killer storms, and there have been Hurricane Hunters flying ever since.

Both Air Force and Navy squadrons now fly regular patrols in both the Atlantic and Pacific, carrying complete meteorological laboratories that constantly monitor the atmosphere around them, in search of the first signs of a developing hurricane or typhoon. Once a storm does blow up, the Hurricane Hunter planes fly repeatedly into, under (as low as 500 feet), and over the vast cloud wall, measuring its size, its wind velocities, its forward speed and course, etc., radioing all this information back to weather stations on the earth.

Hurricane penetration has become routine by now, but it hasn't yet become either safe or pleasant. (A standing joke among the Hurricane Hunters is that a flight into the storm is "like going over Niagara Falls in a telephone booth.") It's a jouncing, jolting trip through clouds and rain so dense that sometimes the fliers cannot see the wingtips of their plane. Sometimes neither the plane nor the fliers are ever seen again.

In 1952, an Air Force plane left the island of Guam to track typhoon Wilma. In 1955, a Navy plane flew into hurricane Janet, carrying a crew of ten, plus two newspapermen looking for a story. In 1958, another Guam-based Air Force plane went up for a survey of typhoon Ophelia. None of these planes ever came back. They vanished silently and without a clue to their fate.

World War II inspired a number of new inventions which, while designed for purposes of offense or defense against a human enemy, turned out to be adaptable as well to man's war against the killer storms. The most revolutionary of these inventions was radar. Basically, it is a means of detecting approaching enemy ships, planes, or missiles at an extremely long distance, by broadcasting radio waves and then, as some of the waves bounce off the objects, catching their "echoes" as glowing blips on a cathode-ray screen.

From the earliest use of radar, however, its operators found that they often ran into interference. If a rainstorm or even a cloud or dense fog lay between them and their target, the water droplets would intercept the radio waves and bounce them back as a blob instead of a blip on the radarscope. This was a maddening nuisance, and a menace, since it screened any enemy attack that might be on the way, until the radarmen learned how to adjust their radio wavelengths so that they ignored the water droplets and didn't bounce until they hit some more solid object.

Meanwhile the meteorologists were delighted to discover that radar could find, pinpoint, and track something as insubstantial and ghostly as a wet piece of atmosphere. As soon as the war ended, they put radar to work doing just that. Since then, radar's sensitivity has been refined and its range extended, so that its screen can "draw" a picture of a hurricane's spiral system when it is still more than 200 miles away, and follow every bend and kink of its course from then on. (Where the Indians once fearfully watched rooster-tail clouds in the sky, Americans watched the approach of hurricane Diane on television when newscasts on the

*When a hurricane or typhoon comes within range of land-based aircraft, the Hurricane Hunters go out to keep an eye on its development and progress. Here the crew of a U.S. Air Force Weather Reconnaissance plane is being briefed before taking off on such a mission.*

U.S. AIR FORCE

night of August 16, 1955, showed them a radarscope portrait of the oncoming storm.)

Another wartime development was the electronic computer. While its contributions to meteorology are not so dramatic as radar's, they are equally important. The computers at the National Meteorological Center at Suitland, Maryland, are occupied with all of America's weather: studying it, analyzing it, and providing the meteorologists with the findings that enable them to forecast the nation's daily weather with an ever-increasing degree of accuracy. But the computers would have proved their worth, if they were used for nothing but storm watching.

As soon as a hurricane is born and detected, the computers are fed the reports that pour in from Hurricane Hunter planes, weather ships, on-shore observers, and radar tracking stations. The machines take in the countless details of temperature, barometric pressures, humidity, wind speeds and directions, and the moment-by-moment changes in these figures—not just those of the storm area, but of all the regions that are or might eventually be in the hurricane's path.

Faster than an army of master mathematicians, the computers can study all these data—taking into account the storm's movements to date, its speed-ups and slow-downs, the air currents in which the storm system is riding, and the basic wave patterns of the atmosphere all over that part of the planet—and they can come up with simplified, straightforward estimates of the various courses the hurricane may take. From these, the meteorologists can make at least an informed guess as to the hurricane's future path and the time it will take to cover it.

So far, the computers only provide the digested data from which the weathermen make the predictions. Distilling all the data into a weather forecast still requires a human brain with training, experience, intuition, and sometimes an inspired hunch.

World War II, which brought the weathermen new equipment and techniques, also forced some changes in their scope and methods of forecasting. For example, the U.S. Weather Bureau had never attempted to set up any network of stations to watch for tornadoes, as it had done for hurricanes. The feeling was that tornadoes were too quick in their build-up and too rapid in their courses for any warning system to do any good. From the 1880's on, the best the Bureau had ever been able to do was to announce at intervals that "conditions are favorable for severe local storms."

But the war brought airfields and troop camps and defense plants to the midwestern states, and the military authorities demanded tornado protection for them. So the Weather Bureau recruited observers all over the midwest, most of them volunteers who could get quickly to a telephone: small town storekeepers, farmers, filling-station workers, switchboard operators. When numerous people had reported a tornado's distance and direction from them, the weathermen could get a "fix" on its position and course, and notify local radio stations to broadcast a warning.

Still the U.S. Weather Bureau wouldn't allow its midwestern offices to use the word "tornado"; the radio broadcasts warned only of "severe local storms." The Air Corps, however, was not so vague. When an air base got one of these reports from the local weather bureau, it frankly warned its service personnel of "tornado weather coming." Since the townspeople around an air base heard these announcements—and ran for shelter when they did—the civilian Weather Bureau eventually followed suit and began bluntly saying "tornadoes" when it meant tornadoes.

The reason for its long-time timidity about the word was that the Weather Bureau had so often been criticized for issuing false alarms. Long before this time, the U.S. Weather Bureau had ceased to concentrate its attention just on farm affairs, as it had done when it was first made an agency of the Department of Agriculture, and had started taking account of the weather's impact on cities, industry, travel, business, American life in general. (Hence, in 1940, it had more realistically been made an agency of the Department of Commerce.) So it had become answerable for its actions to a wide variety of critics.

When it broadcast a storm warning, every activity in the endangered area would come to a halt; people would scurry to shelter, storekeepers would board up their show windows, etc. And if the storm did not materialize, the Weather Bureau would get a storm of its own—complaints from merchants that it had interfered with trade, from schools that it had interrupted classes, from housewives that it had prevented their hanging out the wash to dry, and so on.

The Weather Bureau was hardly at fault. When it spotted tornado weather coming, those storm conditions might extend over an area of 20,000 square miles, and that was the area it warned. If the Bureau simply said "severe local storms" it wasn't sticking its neck out, but if it said "tornadoes" everybody in that area went underground. Then, if just a single tornado funnel dropped down from that expanse of clouds, it would tear up a strip of terrain that might be only four square miles in extent. The people in those four square miles would be grateful for the warning that had sent them to shelter; the people in the other 19,996 square miles would complain that the Weather Bureau had "cried wolf."

The Bureau's hurricane warnings have come in for equal criticism. In 1955, hurricane Ione thrashed northward through the east coast waters of the United States and rolled into the Carolinas at Cape Lookout. In the weathermen's best judgment, that killer storm was going to continue its northward course, right through the heavily built-up metropolitan areas from Washington all the way to New York City and beyond—and the Bureau said so. Since that area had not recovered from the massive devastation of hurricanes Connie and Diane, just a month earlier, the effect of that warning can be imagined.

All through the northeast, Coast Guard ships put to sea, Red Cross and Civil Defense workers were mobilized, Army units were hastily recalled from leave and put on alert. In New York City alone, extra police and firemen were called to duty, airlines cancelled their flights in and out of the city, offices and factories sent their employees home early. Then Ione decided to be satisfied with killing seven people and doing $160,000,000 worth of damage in North Carolina; it turned abruptly eastward and vanished out to sea. Millions of dollars in trade, man-hours, and taxes had been wasted. Everybody in the northeast, from Pentagon generals to school principals, railed at the Weather Bureau for its costly "error" in forecasting.

Nevertheless, the Bureau has wisely decided to continue its policy of "over-warning" when necessary, and hopes that eventually the general public will come to realize that it's better safe than sorry. No one yet has been able to outguess and foretell every single movement of a hurricane or tornado, but the meteorologists' record of accuracy continues to get better and better.

In the early days of the Weather Bureau, only one in four of its forecasts was anywhere near correct. Today, when it makes a

*The Hurricane Hunter plane—this one a WB-47, converted from a bomber to a "flying weather laboratory"—jets off from Florida for a look at a hurricane.*

U.S. AIR FORCE

prediction of the weather to come in the next twelve to eighteen hours, that forecast is accurate 85 percent of the time. A forecast of the weather a day and a half ahead will prove correct three times out of four. As evidence of the Bureau's increasing efficiency, look at some before-and-after figures:

In 1935, when that Labor Day hurricane tore through the Florida Keys, it killed more than four hundred people. Twenty-five years later, when hurricane Donna followed the same track in 1960, there were nine times as many people inhabiting the Keys. But, thanks to the Weather Bureau's warning, which gave them time to evacuate the islands, only three people perished. In 1961, hurricane Carla hit the Texas coast at Galveston, just as that other infamous killer storm had done in 1900. There had been a tremendous increase in population in that area, but the storm warnings came in time for 350,000 people to flee to safer ground. Only twenty-four of them died, and most of those were caught by tornadoes that formed on the fringes of the hurricane.

In 1960, the meteorologists got their most revolutionary new tool since the invention of radar when the first weather-watching satellite went into orbit around the earth and 750 miles above it. The satellite was called Tiros (from the initials of Television Infra-Red Observation Satellite) and during its two and a half months of life, it sent back to earth nearly 20,000 photographs of the planet's surface and its cloud cover. That was man's first look down on the weather over a large segment of his world, and one of the pictures showed the unmistakable spiral twist of a typhoon over the Pacific.

The first Tiros was short-lived and weak-eyed in comparison to the later, more sophisticated satellites that followed it. Tiros III, for instance, stayed in orbit for nearly eight months in 1961, during which time it photographed five hurricanes in the Atlantic and Caribbean, two hurricanes off western Mexico, and nine typhoons in the Pacific. Some of these storms were already known to exist by the time the satellite's orbit brought its cameras over them, but Tiros III gets full credit for spotting one of the weather disturbances before any other observer did. That one turned out to be hurricane Carla, and the satellite's early detection of it was what gave 350,000 Texans time to flee for their lives.

A weather satellite would be worth its multimillion-dollar cost if it did no more than discover one Carla during its whole lifetime aloft. But these orbiting observers do more than watch for a developing killer storm; they monitor it throughout its entire career. Previously, high-flying Hurricane Hunter planes had provided the meteorologists with overhead views of a hurricane's spiral-and-eye formation. The satellites, flying higher yet, can photograph the entire storm and a vast area of its surroundings as well.

From such pictures, the meteorologists can analyze the storm's relation to other weather conditions in existence at the same time. By studying these overall patterns, the weathermen are gradually learning more about the atmospheric elements that breed a "tropical weather disturbance," the conditions which either stunt its growth at that point or encourage its development into a mature hurricane, the forces that steer its erratic course, and the conditions that dissolve it at last.

In 1964, the U.S. Department of Commerce decided that its Weather Bureau meteorologists and other scientists in its other agencies—oceanographers, satellite technicians, seismologists, etc. —could work better if they worked in closer collaboration with each other. It organized the Environmental Science Services Administration, better known as ESSA. This organization concerns itself with every phenomenon of the environment, from stratospheric cosmic rays to underground earthquakes. The Weather Bureau is now a sub-agency of ESSA, as is the Coast & Geodetic Survey, the Experimental Satellite Center and a number of other bureaus. Now closely allied, they work, study, experiment, and swap information (with similar agencies in other countries, too) in an attempt to see the "total picture" of the earth and to understand the forces both inside and outside it.

*An ESSA technician, flying through a hurricane in a DC-6 monitor plane, checks the digital data system which tape-records meteorological observations—temperatures, barometric pressures, wind speeds, etc.—every second during flight.*

*ESSA*

Now the Weather Bureau has a peculiar problem. A meteorologist's main frustration used to be that he could not manipulate in one brain all the numberless details of his daily work: the constantly shifting lines on his charts, the constantly changing figures on temperature, pressure, humidity, etc. The Weather Bureau's complaint today is just the opposite. It is staffed with expert professionals using the most modern equipment. It has at its command electronic computers, Space Age satellites, reconnaissance planes and ships, networks of trained observers and eager volunteers, and the collaboration of its fellow agencies in ESSA. What it doesn't have is enough facts and figures to work with.

The data pour in, reports and statistics from around and over the world. The computers digest them instantaneously, and the meteorologists quickly translate the results into terms that the general public can understand. Then they cry for still more information. For there are large areas of the world that are what the weathermen call data voids—places where there are no observers to watch the weather and report its doings.

Every day's weather everywhere—including every killer storm—is the product of a worldwide pattern of interacting conditions. The existence of just one data void—in the empty middle of some ocean, for instance—means a blank spot on the weatherman's charts, a gap in his calculations and, inevitably, the likelihood of an error in the forecast he has to compile from incomplete information. It is probable that the meteorologists' forecasts will never be 100 percent accurate, 100 percent of the time, because it's unlikely that all of the world's data voids will ever have enough observers stationed in them to observe everything that goes on everywhere in the atmosphere.

There is reason to hope that the weather satellites will eventually be able to do some of that watching. At this moment, there are satellites in orbit observing nearly every inch of the world, and some of them have infra-red eyes that can see and shoot pictures on the night side of the planet. Others carry instruments that can measure the temperature of the atmosphere and the cloud tops. But these space robots have their limitations.

To date, no satellite can measure the varying air pressures several hundred miles below. It cannot judge the wind speeds and directions away down there. It cannot take a temperature reading of less than a wide and general area. It cannot see what's going on underneath the clouds. In short, the robot weather watchers will have to be exceedingly more sensitive and talented before they can replace human observers wielding the simple instruments of Galileo and Torricelli.

Meanwhile, humans cope with the weather, and the storms it brings, as best they can. If the storm-warning systems in the Americas are still not 100 percent perfect, they are the most efficient the world has ever known.

The storm specialists at Miami's National Hurricane Center are constantly studying the photographs that come from space via ESSA's Satellite Center at Suitland, Maryland, the data relayed to them from the computers at the National Meteorological Center, and the reports that come in from Air Force and Navy weather planes and ships. They watch for anything out of the normal—cloud changes, wind shifts, suspicious new patterns in the upper-air waves—anything that may signal a storm in the making.

When a disturbance is suspected, it may be so far out at sea that only the orbiting satellites can keep an eye on it. As soon as the satellite photographs show the beginning of the spiral cloud formation, and as soon as that spiral moves within flying range, Hurricane Hunter planes are sent out to take a look at it. If they verify that a storm exists—and at this stage it probably still is just a "storm" with only moderately fast winds—the Hurricane Center gives it a name (this one can be called Felice), and sends a notice of its existence to the newspapers, radio and television stations. Thereafter, every six hours, the Center issues another bulletin on Felice's progress and development.

The Hurricane Hunter planes, and sometimes weather ships, keep tracking the storm. If it's going to become a hurricane, it usually does so by about the third day, and the Hurricane Hunters find that its central winds are now up to seventy-five miles per hour or more. By now, Felice is approaching the farthest-out islands of the West Indies, and the Hurricane Center flashes a "hurricane warning" to the weather stations there. For the rest of the islands it issues a "small-craft warning." To ships outside the hurricane's immediate area, it broadcasts a "gale warning." To the news media in the United States, the Hurricane Center is still issuing its six-hourly bulletins, forecasting Felice's "probable" march during the next day or so. (Although a hurricane's forward speed at this stage is seldom more than fifteen miles an hour, that means that it can travel as far as 360 miles in a full day.)

As Felice moves across the West Indies, other storm watchers come into action. One is the radar "fence" along the United States coast—weather bureaus from Texas to New England, whose radars have a 200-mile range and whose "sweeps" overlap, providing an unbroken guard line from Tamaulipas, Mexico, around the Gulf and Florida, through the Bahamas, and up the east coast to Portland, Maine.

An auxiliary storm watch is provided by ESSA's Coast & Geodetic Survey stations, which keep a check on the coastal tides from Texas to Massachusetts. These detect the advance sea swell of an approaching hurricane, and help determine where the storm is headed for and how violent its waves are likely to be. Another back-up warning system is that known as CHURN (Cooperative Hurricane Reporting Network), composed of volunteer and amateur weathermen who operate their own private wind and tide measuring equipment and report their observations to their neighborhood Coast Guard stations.

As Felice moves closer to the mainland, the National Hurricane Center's six-hourly bulletins are supplemented with special notices issued as the situation demands. When the storm is within range of the radar fence and its course can be watched every minute, the Center may broadcast a "hurricane watch" for certain areas. This is not a prediction that those areas are going to be hit, but a caution that they may be, and so it alerts their emergency forces to stand ready for action. If Felice is expected to pass far enough away from land that its most violent winds will remain at sea, the Center may issue a gale warning so the coastal areas will expect at least its fringe winds, and the Center may add a note that Felice's fringes can include tornadoes or storm waves.

The Center keeps repeating that hurricane watch notice until and unless it becomes fairly certain that Felice will hit some particular area. Then it changes the hurricane watch to a hurricane warning. The decision to make the change is a delicate one.

A single city like Miami may spend hundreds of thousands of dollars to prepare for a storm—boarding up its windows, tying down boats, mobilizing emergency workers, stocking shelters with food and water. The Center doesn't want to impel this preparation until there is no doubt that it's necessary. On the other hand, if the Center waits too long to declare the emergency, its warning may come too late for the city to prepare. In the meantime, Felice may be wobbling all over the ocean offshore, its own lack of decision making the meteorologists sweat over theirs.

Though an occasional storm is so erratic that the Hurricane Center cannot give more than six hours' notice to the areas it will hit, the usual hurricane warning goes out twelve to sixteen hours ahead of the onslaught. The warning is as complete as it can be. It tells at what time Felice will strike, what its wind speeds will be, what the height of its storm waves will be, when the calm eye can be expected, and when the second blast will come. The bulletin gives an estimate of what kind of damage the winds, rain, and waves will probably do, and suggests emergency procedures to minimize that damage. For communities around Felice's edges, the Center also announces the speeds of the gales they can expect, and advises if tornadoes are accompanying the storm.

When Felice moves inland, it begins to die, though it may do that slowly, over many days. Its winds diminish and its size expands, while its rains may be more torrential than ever. From this point on, while still reporting Felice's direction and progress, the Hurricane Center's bulletins concentrate on warning those areas where there is a danger of floods. Long after Felice has ceased to be technically a hurricane, the Center will keep track of it and keep the people in its path informed of what to expect.

The National Severe Storms Forecast Center at Kansas City, Missouri, operates much the same as does the Hurricane Center, except that it has less time in which to watch its storms' buildup and track their courses. The NSSFC works with the tornadoes of the midwest. Satellites cannot spot them because they almost always occur on the under side of a heavy cloud layer, and they're here and gone before a satellite could transmit a photograph to earth. The meteorologists of the NSSFC can recognize weather conditions that are likely to breed tornadoes—when they do, they broadcast warnings to the affected areas of the country—but the first alert they get of a twister doesn't come until somebody sees the thing.

So far, there is no device or technique that can predict a tornado's time and place of arrival until it appears. Not even radar has been of much help. Aimed directly at an actual tornado funnel in plain sight, the radar can sometimes distinguish it from the mass of stormy clouds from which it dangles. But radar can't always do even that. To its radio waves, clouds are clouds, and the one that's a spinning killer seems no different from the merely ugly ones.

However, a recent development called "Doppler radar" may turn out to be more discriminating. Unlike other radar, it does not measure a target's size or distance, but the speed with which it moves. When Doppler radar is trained on a bank of clouds, it may detect the rapid whirl of water droplets high up where the tornado winds start their spin, and may do it at least a few precious minutes before the funnel starts to snake down to the ground.

Until Doppler radar or some other invention can do that, the earliest and best warning system consists of human observers throughout the nation keeping a wary eye on the sky. Already there are several thousand volunteer citizens in the midwest's "tornado alley," reporting by telephone to some five hundred local weather offices. In 1969 the U.S. Weather Bureau announced that it hopes to recruit many more volunteers to help staff a program it calls "Skywarn." In addition to stationing a greater number of tornado spotters all over the country, Skywarn stresses a preparedness drive in which Civil Defense and Red Cross workers participate, teaching the residents of tornado areas how to brace themselves for the blow before it comes, how to live through it, and how to pick up the pieces afterward.

# 9
# YOU AND THE
# KILLER STORMS

If you live in South America or Alaska or in the middle of Africa or on the equator or in the far north of Canada or Russia, you can skip this chapter, because you're unlikely to encounter either a hurricane, a typhoon, or a tornado. If you live or visit or spend holidays in any other part of the world, or expect to sometime, this chapter may save your life or help you save someone else's.

By now, having read this far, you know a great deal about the killer storms, and you probably have a good idea of their dangers. This chapter will tell you how best to avoid those dangers and how to minimize the ones that are unavoidable. If and when you do find yourself in a killer storm, you may very well be more helpful— certainly less helpless—than others who haven't bothered to acquire that knowledge.

Recently the Environmental Science Services Administration did a study of their various warning systems and found, somewhat discouragingly, that their warnings were more efficient than the people who were warned. It appears that people who grow up without experiencing a killer storm feel that "it hasn't happened before and it won't this time"—even when their radio is advising that a storm is on the way to their town. ESSA's report goes on to say that although some people take the trouble to learn what to do in a killer storm, if the storm doesn't come along right away they quickly forget what they have learned. Then, when a disaster does occur, they act as surprised and disorganized as chickens attacked by a hawk.

It may be years before you meet a killer storm, if ever, but the do's and don't's of coping with it are not difficult, and chances are that you'll remember them when they are needed. This is not to say that you should try to take charge of your whole town when disaster strikes, or make a pest of yourself as a know-it-all. But if you can help or advise in even the smallest way, you'll be doing yourself, your family, and perhaps your neighbors a deal of good.

For example, when a hurricane is on the way, a family's first impulse is to shut up the house like a fortress and barricade it from the inside, with every single crack sealed so that not even a drop of rain will get in to wet the carpet. If you quietly suggest that a window should be left open—and explain why—you may be saving that house from far worse damage than a damp carpet.

ESSA publishes a pamphlet entitled *The Greatest Storm on Earth . . . HURRICANE,* in which it describes an imaginary seaside city called Homeport, whose citizens are alert and aware of their danger and have taken long-range measures to guard against it. The first thing the Homeporters did was to set up a permanent Hurricane Committee, consisting of a number of their own city officials, their Civil Defense chief, officials of disaster-relief agencies, their police and fire chiefs, the local newspaper publishers, the managers of the city's radio and television stations, officials from the water and power companies, and representatives sent to advise them by the State and Federal governments.

This committee began by studying all the hazards of a hurricane, then deciding which of them would most affect Homeport. For one thing, they realized that a storm wave would inundate low-lying portions of the city, in one of which was situated the water supply plant. Even if the storm wave did not interrupt the supply, its salt could contaminate the water and make it unfit to use. So Homeport built an auxiliary plant on higher ground, big enough to supply clean drinking water for as long as it would take to get the regular plant into operation again.

The committee also designated one well-sheltered building as an emergency center from which all of the city's operations could be directed—a combination City Hall, police and fire headquarters —with its own electric generator and telephones in case the city's main power and communications lines should fail. Other stout buildings were designated as emergency shelters for storm refugees, and stocked with food, water, bedding, and medical supplies. In case of a really bad storm, Homeport's Hurricane Committee asked other towns, farther inland, to be ready to provide similar shelters should its citizens have to flee.

To expedite any necessary mass evacuation, Homeport's city engineer mapped the areas from which people would be moved at a first alarm, a second alarm, etc. The police mapped the best evacuation routes and made plans to deal with the traffic flow. The Committee compiled a list of volunteers who owned airplanes, boats, and "ham" radio sets, who would act as emergency res-cuers, messengers, or communicators with the outside world. The Committee meets every May, just before the start of the storm season, to review its preparedness plans and make any changes or improvements necessary. Then, every month from June through November, it checks its emergency equipment, communications systems, and the stockpiles of food and necessities.

Some other (real) cities go even further in their preparations than the fictional Homeport. Miami has a strict building code that does not allow the erection of any structure not designed to withstand hurricane winds and waves. It is obvious that a flimsily built house can go to pieces and injure its occupants, but the Miami authorities are just as concerned about their other citizens outside that house, who might be hurt by its flying fragments.

Still other communities realize that modern man has built hazards for himself that earlier civilizations in the storm areas didn't have to worry about. These farsighted towns make the power companies lay their cables underground, because a storm can snap exposed wires and flail them about, spitting death-dealing electricity. Even when their power is shut off, the broken lines are wild whips capable of slashing and killing.

Some towns ban billboards. In a storm, the billboards are usually the first structures to go down. Either their planks or metal sheets become separate missiles or the billboards themselves fly away like giant guillotine blades, capable of cutting off a man's head or slicing away the top storey of a house with equal ease. Other towns restrict the kind and placement of store signs. Wood and metal ones can come crashing down on the street below. Certain signs made of glowing glass tubing have a built-in danger all their own. When they smash, their glass becomes a flying spray of shrapnel; but, worse, some of these tubings have a fluoride or phosphor coating on their glass. If one of their splinters merely scratches a person he risks an infection that's always difficult to cure and can be fatal.

Almost all of these community safeguards would be logical precautions to take against any kind of storm, whether the outright killers like hurricanes, typhoons, and tornadoes or just worse-than-usual thunderstorms and windstorms. Likewise, most of the long-range preparations suggested for private homes provide protection against a wide variety of disasters.

Every home, whether house or apartment, should keep on hand a stock of emergency foods, cooking equipment, sanitary facilities, first-aid supplies, a battery-powered radio, and flashlights or lanterns. In a house, if there's any chance of floods in the area, all these should be stored on the uppermost floor.

Every home should have basic fire-fighting equipment: an extinguisher or at least a pail of sand kept handy on each floor. Water faucets in the kitchen, laundry, or bathroom should have screw-on adapters so that a garden hose can be attached to them for use indoors. All household fuels and other flammable liquids should be stored outside the house.

In every family, at least one adult should have first-aid training. Such courses are usually available, free of cost, at the nearest headquarters of Civil Defense, the YMCA, or the Red Cross. For boys and girls, Scout training is most heartily recommended. Both the Boy and Girl Scouts provide excellent first-aid courses.

If your family lives in a neighborhood subject to storm waves or floods, its adult members ought to be familiar with the shortest and safest route out of that area and onto higher ground. The family automobile, if not kept in a garage, should be under some kind of shelter (but *not* under trees). In areas liable to flooding, the car should be parked on the highest part of the family property. Its gas tank ought always to be as nearly full as possible.

If there are trees around your house, they should be kept pruned of dead branches, which they will shed with vicious force in the first storm wind, and also of any branches extending near the house, which could smash in windows, rip off gutters and drainpipes, or batter at the roof and walls.

If you live in a hurricane area, and your house isn't stormproof, there is probably a public shelter within reach and you'll have time to reach it. If you live in tornado country, your family ought to have a shelter of its own, as a twister comes too fast for you to flee far. Midwesterners have learned to dig underground storm cellars somewhere on their property, well away from any possible falling objects. The doors of such a cellar should open inward, so that if something does get thrown across them the occupants

won't be trapped inside. However, in case the cellar should somehow be sealed under debris, it ought to have a ventilating system
and a stock of food, water, first-aid supplies, and battery-power
lighting, enough to last the occupants for a day or so, until the
neighbors discover their predicament and free them.

About the only other ahead-of-time precaution that can be taken
against a tornado is the practice of leaving a window or a ventilator
louver of your house open at all times. Thus, if you're not at home
when the storm comes, the house will stand a better chance of not
blowing itself up from internal air pressure.

There is unfortunately very little that you can do about protecting your own person if a tornado swoops down on you outdoors.
Despite the best efforts of the Weather Bureau, the Severe Storms
Forecast Center, and ESSA as a whole, there is still no warning
system that can alert every single citizen to his danger far enough
ahead of time for him to seek shelter. The twister doesn't *allow*
enough time. Probably the first you will hear of it is the funnel
cloud's own spine-chilling roar.

You'll have some chance of escape if you remember a couple of
basic facts about the tornado. It is probably stalking forward at
about forty-five miles per hour, which means you can't outrun it on
foot in the same direction. But in the midwestern United States its
general movement is from the southwest towards the northeast. So
your best bet is to run at right angles to that path, in other words,
run either southeast or northwest.

An automobile can outrun a twister, if the driver sees it in time,
and has plenty of road to run on. However, a car is the very worst
place to be caught by a tornado (the next worst is a house trailer
or mobile home that's not firmly anchored down), because a
twister that can pick up a steam locomotive can obviously do what
it likes with any smaller vehicle—and what it does is usually something horrible. If you are in a car and a tornado is about to over-
take it, you'll be safer to stop the car, run as far from it as possible,
and lie face down in a roadside ditch.

The best place to sit out a tornado is as far underground as you can get. This means your storm cellar (or anybody's) if you can reach it in time. The next best shelter is a building's basement. When you get there, crouch in the southwest corner of it, so that you have the angle of the wall, and all the earth behind it, between you and the twister's first hammer blow.

If you can't get underground, duck into the nearest heavily-constructed building: one of reinforced concrete or steel framing. Do not, however, pick any great sprawling arena like an auditorium, supermarket, or even a movie theater. Their roofs have to cover a wide area, usually with little interior support, so they are liable to collapse. Don't run into an ordinary family-style frame or brick house, just because it's there. It won't be there for long. If nothing better is in sight, find a ditch, a gully, any slightest depression in the earth, throw yourself face down and hug the ground for all you're worth.

That's all. That's all anyone can tell you about defending yourself from a tornado, except perhaps to add "Good luck!" At least the instructions are so few and simple that they are easy to remember. Remembering them, you'll stand a chance of staying alive.

Let's get back, then, to the killer storm that we *can* more or less prepare for—the hurricane or typhoon.

When you are laying in emergency supplies for use during a hurricane (or to live on after a tornado), that stock-up requires some forethought. The kind of groceries to stock should meet three requirements: they mustn't need refrigeration, they should be edible without cooking or with very little, and they should not be thirst-making in case you run short of water. This means you should stock things like canned tuna fish and luncheon meats, to be eaten with crackers (they stay fresh in their wax-paper wrappers), with canned fruits and chocolate bars for dessert (and for their sugar energy). Also lay in a supply of paper plates and cups, and plastic knives, forks, and spoons. These won't waste precious water in having to be washed.

If you want to have hot meals during the storm, and maybe for a while afterward, you will need emergency cooking equipment on the order of a gasoline camp stove. Such equipment should not just be stored away until it's needed, for if it is not checked over and cleaned occasionally, it can cause an explosion when it's lighted.

One thing that many "disaster handbooks" neglect to mention is sanitary facilities. This means having some kind of covered pail, and paper or plastic bags or liners for it, in which to deposit human wastes. Because, if the water supply fails in your house, the toilets are not going to flush. The emergency facility, using bags that can be disposed of outside the house, will spare the family at least an uncomfortable and embarrassing nuisance, and perhaps the risk of spreading disease.

Another thing that the disaster manuals overlook is the matter of household pets. The dog, the cat, and any other pets will have to be taken indoors with the family. If there is any risk that the family may have to flee to a public shelter, you should have made some other arrangement for the pets ahead of time. Animals can-not be allowed inside a public shelter that may be crammed with people. Perhaps, at the first announcement of a hurricane warning, you would want to move your pets to some friend's more solidly-built house or to a safe boarding kennel.

For your own house, emergency lighting equipment is a must. Stock candles for a last resort, but kerosene lamps are both brighter and safer. Best are flashlights or electric lanterns, in case you have to be out in the wind after dark. Stock plenty of spare bulbs and bat-teries for them; check the batteries at intervals and replace them when they seem weak. A battery-powered radio is another must. Your town's electricity may fail quite early in the storm, and your regular radio and television will be dead from then on. Without a battery radio, you would be cut off from all further storm bulletins when you need them most.

A lot of families hesitate to stock emergency supplies because they fear being ridiculed by their friends and neighbors as "timid souls." They also reason that all those supplies are within easy reach at the nearby shopping center; why clutter up the house with them before they're needed? But then, when the first hurricane watch is broadcast, nobody fears ridicule; there is a run on those supplies and it's everyone for himself. Long before the hurricane watch has been changed to a hurricane warning, you won't find a flashlight battery or a candle in any store in town.

As was explained in the previous chapter, a hurricane watch does not mean that a storm is coming, but only that it might. The people in the alerted areas are merely advised to keep their television or radio tuned in for further bulletins, and to be ready to start emergency procedures if the watch should be changed to a warning. There is as yet no cause at all for panic, or even for hurrying, but there *are* a couple of preparations that your family might undertake at this stage.

It's a good time to fill up the car's tank with gasoline. If and when the hurricane warning comes, there will be a rush on the filling stations. Even after the storm has gone, the gas stations may be closed, either flooded out or crippled by a power failure.

This is also a good time to lay in an emergency water supply, filling every large, clean jar, jug, bottle, and container in the house—even the bathtub, after sterilizing it with boiling water. Your town's water may be contaminated by flooding—the salt water of a storm wave can get into it, or sewers may overflow into it—or the supply may be cut off entirely if a power failure stops the pumps.

You are drawing your water early, and so will other sensible families, for a better reason than over-cautiousness. Eventually, nearly every house in town will want to stock up on water, but if they were all to turn on their taps at the last minute, that could cause a disaster. The pressure in the water mains would be so reduced that, in case of a fire's breaking out somewhere in town, the firemen's hoses would dribble instead of gush.

There's nothing more to do now until and unless the hurricane watch is changed to a hurricane warning. Your whole family should be ready to swing into action when that happens. The weatherman will try to issue that warning a day ahead of the storm's arrival in your area. But a really dodgy storm can keep the weathermen guessing until it picks a target. So your warning may come no more than six hours ahead. That's just 360 minutes, and they can seem frightfully short when there's a killer coming on the 361st.

If you live in typhoon territory—India, the Philippines, Japan, or elsewhere in the Orient—you can seldom expect any warning at all. The Far Eastern countries have not developed storm watching or warning systems comparable to America's. In those places the only alert may be a weather station's hoisting of the internationally-recognized hurricane flags—two bright red flags with square black centers or, at night, a red lantern between two white lanterns.

If your family has to move out of the storm's way, now is the time to do it. If you are living or vacationing along a low-lying beach, and the hurricane warning says that "exposed coastal areas should be evacuated"—*get out,* and get out fast. Storm tides often start rising long before the storm hits; if you are not immediately washed away, all the roads to safe places may be. Or a delay in starting can mean that your car gets trapped in a traffic jam.

This is why the driver of a family car should plan and know his getaway route in advance, and if possible have an alternate in mind. If the traffic begins to thicken and slow, he should notice it in time to swing off onto his second-choice road. In case there is no alternate, and traffic does come to a standstill, the driver should have kept in mind, as he passed it, the nearest shelter of any kind that can be reached on foot. A roadside restaurant, a garage, a private house, any halfway sturdy building is better than being caught on a beach road in a car.

If your house is not in a coastal area, you won't have to flee the storm wave; your main concern will be the hurricane's wind and rain. When the hurricane warning is announced, your family's first move should be to protect the windows of your house. Small panes of glass may be shattered by flying debris, and the wind by itself can smash the large panes of picture windows. All should be covered with storm shutters or boarded over or at least strengthened with tape. Do this job before anything else, because shutters or boards will be almost impossible to handle once the wind starts rising. A wise householder will use good heavy lumber for the boarding up, and attach it firmly to the building, because flimsy wood or insecure shutters can blow loose and cause more damage than no shutters at all.

Next, scout your yard and porches for any objects that can be blown about: garden furniture and tools, the porch swing, the garbage cans out back, the toys scattered on the lawn. Carry indoors everything that can be carried, and anchor down everything else.

If your house uses gas for cooking or heating, it should now be turned off at the main inlet. All electrical appliances except the most necessary—the refrigerator, freezer, radio, television—should be disconnected. The dials of the refrigerator and freezer should be turned to their coldest. One thing to be sure to turn off is the water heater, whether it's gas or electric. If the water supply fails, leaving just a puddle in the heater's tank, it can boil up a steam pressure that might result in a violent explosion. If you try the water faucets in the house at any time during the storm and find they have gone dry, don't leave them open. The water will come back on eventually, and if there's nobody home at the time, you could have an indoor flood all your own.

By now, either the wind is already blowing or the bulletins on the radio will tell you from which direction it will come. On the lee side of the house (the side out of the wind), open at least one window part way—several windows if it's a big house. You do this for much the same reason that you would in a tornado. When the fiercest winds come, they are going to get into your house no matter how securely it is barricaded; they'll search out the tiniest cracks.

Though you may not feel it, there will be pressure building up inside the house; if it has no exit handy it can pop out windowpanes or even lift the roof.

Now that you have made the house (or apartment) as storm-ready as possible, it's time to decide whether it is safe enough to sit out the storm in. If there's any doubt about that, the family should vacate, well ahead of the storm, and move to whatever public shelter has been provided by the town. But once the decision has been made to stay at home, *stay there.* Unless the building actually starts to come down you're safer there than trying to flee through the outdoors. On foot or in a car, you would have to dodge hurtling debris, falling trees, showers of broken glass, lashing power lines— and you wouldn't stand much chance of dodging all of them.

In the house, keep a battery-powered radio turned on for further weather bulletins. Stay well away from all windows. When it's time to eat, use up the food in the freezer and refrigerator first, and don't open their doors oftener than necessary. If the power fails and you have to use candles or oil lamps for light, be careful with them; the house will be gusty with drafts of air that can blow them over and start a fire.

It wouldn't seem so, in all that wind and rain, but fire is an ever present danger in a hurricane. An occasional freak storm will bring little or no rain at all. And there are some fires—at a broken gas main, for instance—that will burn fiercely no matter how heavy the downpour of rain. There is every possibility that a hurricane can overturn a gasoline truck or an oil storage tank and then ignite it with a spark-spitting broken power line. While you can't prevent things like that, you can see to it that a fire doesn't start in your own home.

And now . . . simply wait out the storm, keeping calm yourself and doing whatever you can to cheer up the younger or more frightened members of the household. This is, after all, something of an adventure, and one that not everybody experiences. When it's over, and you tell about it to friends who weren't there, you will probably find that they envy your having had the excitement, the danger, and the suspense.

Remember one more thing. If your community is in the path of the hurricane's eye, there will come a time when the storm seems to be over. Of course, everybody should know what the eye is and what it portends; but, as we've observed in storm after storm, not everybody does. *You do.* Don't let it trick you or anyone else in the family into thinking that everything is back to normal. This is only the lull, and the radio bulletins will tell you so, but not even they can tell you exactly how long it will last. The calm may endure for an hour or more, but for safety's sake don't count on more than minutes. There is a second blast coming, from the opposite direction, and it may be worse than the first.

If an emergency repair has to be made—perhaps tightening a loosened storm shutter—it should be done as quickly as possible, and no one allowed outdoors longer than absolutely necessary. There is, however, one change in arrangements that *has* to be done during this lull. Since the wind is going to shift, whatever windows had previously been open on the lee side of the house should now be closed, and others opened up on the opposite side.

Finally the storm is over, but the danger is not. Along coastal areas, storm waves and tides may continue to batter the lowlands long after the hurricane has moved on. Inland, swollen rivers may not disgorge their floods until days after the storm. Anywhere, the hurricane's departing cloud may trail tornadoes in its wake. You must remain alert to the radio bulletins that can warn you of these hazards.

There can be other, local perils lurking in your area that the weathermen and the radio newsmen don't know about. Remember some of the peculiar hazards that other storms have left behind—the burning magnesium barrels that hurricane Diane set afloat in Connecticut, and the potentially poisonous chlorine drums that hurricane Beulah sank in the Mississippi River. There is simply no guessing what kind of booby trap the next killer storm may set before it departs.

After any of the killer storms, your own home street can be full of pitfalls, from ankle-turning rubble underfoot to precariously balanced trees overhead, ready to topple, and tangles of wires that may still be carrying high-voltage electricity. The family car should definitely not be taken out until the streets have been cleaned up. The least that it risks is tire punctures from glass fragments, and it *can* disappear entirely if a street that looks safe on the surface has been undercut by flood waters or broken water mains.

If you have some special skill or training, there may be some useful work that you can do in helping your town dig out from under the storm damage. If you're a Boy or Girl Scout, your troop has probably already been assigned some after-storm job to do.

For example, in past disasters, Girl Scouts have acted as messengers, have made sandwiches in the public shelters, have organized games and other recreation for the refugee children in the storm shelters, have helped receive the injured at medical centers, have sorted shipments of relief clothing, and have baby-sat with the children of adults who were on rescue duty.

The Boy Scouts have helped direct traffic, given house-to-house warnings in an area where gas was escaping from broken mains, helped search for missing persons, bailed out basements, and helped pile sandbags on flood levees and dikes. After a tornado in Massachusetts in 1953, two Scouts used their camping tent to rig a temporary roof for the torn-up home of two old ladies who couldn't be persuaded to leave it. After hurricane Carla hit Texas in 1961, Boy Scouts helped cowboys drag drowned cattle out of the bayous and burn their carcasses.

If you are not a member of a Scout troop or some other organized youth group, but think your services could be of use—for instance, if you're an exper at first aid or an experienced "ham" radio operator—you should mention this, well in advance of any storm, to your local Civil Defense office, the Salvation Army, or the Red Cross, all of which keep files of such special talents and will assign you to duty when you are needed.

Otherwise, if no one in your family is on call for such duty, and unless someone is injured or ill and has to be taken out for medical attention, you will all do the most good to yourselves and others if you simply stay at home for a reasonable time after the storm.

There may already be two kinds of people on the streets who shouldn't be. One is the sightseer, usually from some other neighborhood or town that wasn't touched by the storm. His presence hampers rescue and clean-up workers, and his car impedes the necessary traffic of fire trucks and ambulances.

The other kind of loiterer on the streets is even worse. He is the looter, who combs a disaster area while its residents are still shocked helpless, and picks up whatever valuables he can. His crime would be ugly enough if he merely stole the goods that he finds strewn about. But he will break into undamaged homes and stores as well, figuring that his depredations will be blamed on the storm. He has even been know to strip jewelry from dead bodies. So many of these human vultures have gathered after certain disasters that the authorities have ordered every looter shot on sight.

If you *have* to be on the streets after a storm and you should come upon a looter, do not try any heroics. He is a criminal of the most loathsome sort, and he will react like one. If he has been looting a liquor store he may be dangerously drunk as well. He knows that he may be under the automatic death sentence of being shot on sight, which makes him desperate enough to do anything. Don't let him see you, and get away as soon as you can do so unobserved. Then, at a safe distance, report what you have seen to a policeman or other person in authority.

Also, while you're out, if you should happen to spot someone injured, trapped, or unconscious, the best thing you can do for him is to run for help. An unconscious person may have been felled by a live power line, and he may be lying on it right now; when you touch him, you too will be instantly unconscious or dead. If you find someone trapped under fallen debris, your singlehanded attempts to extricate him may bring down still more rubble and either bury him deeper or trap you with him. If you find a person helplessly injured, unless you are an *expert* at first aid, go looking for someone who is.

If you and the rest of your family are doing the most sensible thing—staying close to home—there are still precautions to be observed. The supply of both water and electricity may be cut off for quite a while. As long as you have to use candles or lamps for light, be very careful of their open flames. If your house catches fire now, neither the fire alarm nor the telephone may be working. When an alarm does get through to the firehouse, it could be a long time before help arrives, because the streets may be too littered for the fire engines to get through. Then, when they finally reach you, the water supply may be too inadequate for them to do any good.

Chances are that the whole town will be suffering from the same breakdown of utilities, but it may be that the mains and cables are damaged only in your area. As soon as the telephone is working, or as soon as it's safe to go out, you will be doing yourself and the utility companies a favor if you report whatever services are still lacking, plus any wires down in your neighborhood, gushing water mains, overflowing sewers, or the smell of a suspected gas leak.

Meantime, keep listening to your radio. It will bring warnings of any floods or tornadoes yet to come, or it may issue other helpful reports and instructions. For example, when your water does start running again, there is a possibility that it may by now be brackish or suspected of contamination. If so, the newscasts will warn you to boil the water before using it. You will want to keep listening to the radio, anyhow, to hear at last the "All clear!" news that the killer storm has finally passed.

# 10
## MAN STRIKES BACK

Of the ten million things that are going on in the world at the moment a man wakes up, the weather is the one that will initially set the course of his day, and it is shaping the other 9,999,999 world happenings as well. It determines whether the farmer will plant that day, whether a housewife will go out to shop, whether a general will start a battle, whether a department store will advertise bathing suits or umbrellas, whether a statesman will make a speech and whether anyone will turn out to hear it, whether highway traffic will be heavy or sparse, whether a space vehicle will be launched toward another planet. . . .

And through all of man's history, of all the ten million daily influences which shaped that history, the one that he has never been able to do a thing about was the weather. But he has tried.

Herodotus, a Greek historian who lived 2,400 years ago, tells of one such attempt in his time: "The storm lasted three days. At last, by offering victims to the winds, and charming them with the help of conjurors, the Magicians succeeded in laying the storm." Then Herodotus adds: "Or perhaps it ceased of its own accord."

In the first years of the Christian era, the Roman Emperor Tiberius would put a wreath made of laurel leaves on his head every time a storm came up, in the belief that lightning would never touch that plant. In other countries and other times, wearing a blossom of hyacinth was supposed to bestow the same protection.

During the Middle Ages, it was believed that Satan's devils caused storms, and that the demons could be frightened away by the sound of good Christian church bells. So, whenever a storm blew up, the bellringers would climb into every church steeple and start hauling on the bell ropes. It was the most foolish thing they could have done, as the steeples were the highest structures in town and the likeliest to attract lightning bolts. In some European towns the church bells were still rung during every storm as recently as the late years of the nineteenth century.

In the West Indies, when the god Hurakán was rampaging around the islands, the natives would cower in their huts, beating drums and shaking rattles in the hope of scaring him away. Later, the Spanish colonists in the islands did very much the same thing. In the belief that Satan was to blame for the hurricane, the priests would parade through the streets carrying crosses and other holy objects intended to fend him off. Then they would lead their church congregations in chanting prayers—the *adrepellendas tempestates* —especially composed by the Vatican for "the arresting of tempests." Meantime, every house and ship in the islands hung up a "cord of St. Francis," a rope tied into three knots of three turns apiece, whose function was to "bind the winds."

In 1880, an American in the midwest invented an "anti-tornado" device. It was to consist of high poles erected all around a town, each pole topped with a bomb. As a twister approached, the bomb or bombs directly in its path would be set off by an electric signal, thus chopping down the tornado funnel like a cornstalk, or so hoped the inventor. The U.S. Patent Office awarded the man his patent, but there is no evidence that his invention was ever actually tested anywhere. (It wouldn't have worked.)

Besides trying to fend off storms, man has often tried to bring some good weather, especially rain for his crops in time of drought. In the Mediterranean countries, after a long dry spell, the people used to bring the statues of saints out of their churches and stand them in the sun, hoping the saints would get so blistered that they would summon up rain in self-defense.

During the four years of the Civil War in the United States, the eastern part of the country complained that it was being drenched by an unusual amount of rain. There was a general belief that the untypical rainfall had been brought on by the incessant concussion of cannon bombardments. Therefore, a few years later, when the Midwest was stricken by a long drought, numerous people wrote to the Weather Service to suggest that it get the Army to fire off several hundred cannon all at once and see if the big boom would again bring rain. The Service's chief commended that such a cannonade would do about as much good as "booing a blizzard or saluting a hailstorm."

Nevertheless, in 1891, when the Midwest was again parched and suffering, the Department of Agriculture did try a similar experiment in Texas. It sent up several hundred kites into the sky, each with a half-pound stick of dynamite tied to its tail, and fired these with electric wires that ran up the kite strings. At two places in Texas, rain did fall after the series of explosions, but the skies had already been cloudy in both areas and no one could prove that the rain wouldn't have fallen anyway.

From the 1890's until about the time of World War II, the Midwestern prairies were prowled by professional "rainmakers." These "professors"—they almost invariably took that title—traveled from place to place, and in the bed of their wagons and trucks there was usually a machine designed to spout impressively colored smoke upward at the sky. When the professor found a drought-stricken neighborhood, and could get the local farmers to pay him for rain, he would unlimber his machine and go to work.

The rainmakers made out all right because they were simply shrewd amateur weathermen. A professor would never set up in business in a locality unless he had studied the weather signs and satisfied himself that rain was already in the offing. Then he would haggle with the local farmers' associations until he figured the rain was due. Then he'd quickly settle the terms and start stoking the rainmaking machine. The next few hours would prove whether he had guessed right or not. Since the rainmakers seldom charged a fee unless the rain *did* fall, their frequent failures were soon forgotten and their occasional successes were widely talked about. A professor with a good weather eye (and good luck) would soon get a good reputation and be in demand all over the Midwest.

When the atomic bomb first came into being, it began to get a lot of the blame for bad weather, just as Hurakán and Satan had once been blamed. Some people, impressed by pictures of the atomic bomb's awesome mushroom cloud, suggested that in peacetime the bomb might be dropped into hurricanes to "break them up."

The scientists, however, knew that the nuclear concussion alone could have no noticeable effect on the weather, either for good or ill. Trying to stop a hurricane with an atomic bomb would be like trying to stop an elephant stampede with a B-B gun. (Just an ordinary summer thunderstorm packs the energy of ten atomic bombs of the size that were dropped on Japan.) Even when the hydrogen bomb was developed—hundreds of times more powerful than the atomic bomb—meteorologists knew that its blast *by itself* could not affect the weather.

They did worry, though, about some other forces let loose during the long series of American and Russian hydrogen-bomb tests in the 1950's. The weathermen wondered if the furious wave of heat that boiled upward from a nuclear explosion might have long-term effects on the temperature of the upper atmosphere. They wondered if the dust kicked up by a bomb test on land, or the water vapor from a test at sea, might billow skyward and become "unnatural" clouds that could alter the normal distribution of sunshine around the earth. They wondered if the radioactivity poured into the atmosphere could upset the balance of the air's natural electric fields.

However, during the tests and afterward, the world's weather seemed no more or less contrary than ever. It appears that not a single one of man's more sensational experiments, from those 1880 "anti-tornado" traps to the biggest hydrogen bomb ever tested, has even been noticed by the much greater forces of the weather. But the weather *has* been affected by one small, seemingly insignificant, totally accidental experiment that took place in the early 1940's. It began with a man blowing his breath into an ordinary kitchen freezer to watch it form a cloud. It may end with our being able to kill the killer storms.

At that time, Vincent J. Schaefer, a molecular physicist, was engaged in research on the phenomenon known as the "supercooled cloud." This is a cloud that seems to break several rules of weather behavior. It is composed of ordinary water vapor, like any other cloud, but although its temperature is well below freezing, often below zero, the vapor obstinately refuses for a long time to freeze into the ice particles which should then collect other droplets and become heavy enough to fall. The vapor simply hangs there, the droplets too small and too light to fall, longer than any explanation could account for. Then, suddenly, as if having made up its mind at last, the vapor does unexpectedly freeze, merge, and fall. Schaefer was trying to find out why the supercooled cloud persists for so long in remaining a cloud, and what is the sudden impetus that turns it into snowflakes.

He studied the supercooled cloud by making one of his own. He lined an ordinary home freezer with black velvet, and trained a bright light and a microscope on the interior. He turned the freezer down to zero temperature and simply blew into it, making a puff of cloud. Then he peered at the little cloud through his microscope, waiting to see the ice crystals eventually form. But his cloud proved even more stubborn than those in the sky; it refused to freeze at all, no matter how long he hovered over it.

Schaefer decided that the ice-making impetus must come from some outside agency; perhaps the dust in the atmosphere. He tried sprinkling the clouds with every kind of dust from quartz and carbon to talcum power and sugar, but none of them would nudge the water vapor into starting to freeze. After months of trying—and quite by accident—he found the substance that would.

It was a hot July day, so hot that his freezer could not cool down to zero. To help lower the temperature, Schaefer dropped into the bottom of the box a chunk of dry ice—frozen carbon dioxide gas—and suddenly he had a miniature snowstorm inside the freezer. The dry ice had lowered the vapor's temperature to the critical point (39 degrees below zero Centigrade) at which a supercooled cloud "makes up its mind" to turn into ice crystals.

By 1946, other experimenters were working on supercooled clouds in the sky, "seeding" them from airplanes with pellets of dry ice, and they confirmed what Schaefer had done in his kitchen freezer. A single piece of dry ice the size of a grain of rice, dropped into such a cloud, would trigger the formation of more than a *trillion* microscopic ice crystals. These, as expected, would become the solid nuclei around which other water droplets gathered, and finally each would become a crystal heavy enough to fall from the cloud. Depending on the temperature of the lower air, the fall would either be snow or would melt on the way down and hit the ground as rain.

Within another year the dry-ice method was already outmoded. By 1947, other scientists had found what Vincent Schaefer had first sought—the solid substance or sublimation nucleus that would attract water molecules together into a crystal or droplet heavy enough to fall. This substance is the chemical silver iodide. It's the ideal sublimation nucleus because the molecular structure of its crystals is so similar to that of water-ice crystals themselves. And it has one big advantage over dry ice in seeding clouds.

The dry-ice method works by cooling the cloud's vapor to that critical $-39°$ C. at which some droplets within the cloud freeze and themselves become solid nuclei. Silver iodide crystals, sprinkled into a cloud, start the vapor-crystallizing process at a considerably higher temperature ($-4°$ C.). Therefore the cloud doesn't have to be one of the infrequent supercooled type. Silver iodide can force a rain- or snowfall out of an ordinary cloud, provided it is sufficiently heavy with water vapor.

However, even with the seeding technique, man still doesn't really *make* rain; he just makes it *fall*. The rain has to be already up there, in the form of clouds of water vapor, and all that man does with his sprinkling of dry ice or silver iodide is to prod the clouds into letting the water loose. But being able to do that does give man an important degree of mastery over the weather.

No sooner had the seeding technique been discovered than meteorologists started asking themselves: could this "rainmaking" method possibly be used to tame a hurricane? Was it possible that seeding a killer storm might make it expend all its terrible energy, not in its usual fearsome winds but perhaps in one vast disgorgement of rain, and make it do that harmlessly, far at sea?

In October, 1947, the U.S. Weather Bureau made its first try at just such an experiment, with "Project Cirrus." An airplane was sent to seed a hurricane which, at the time, was well out at sea off the coast of Florida. The plane sprinkled dry ice into the cloud wall around the hurricane's eye (the silver iodide method had not yet come into general use), while the meteorologists watched.

The hurricane, which had been on a northeasterly course that probably would have kept it clear of land, immediately made a sharp swerve westward and smashed into the coast just south of Savannah, Georgia. It wasn't one of the worst hurricanes—only one man was killed (by a falling tree), but from the Carolinas to Florida, the storm did some twenty-four million dollars' worth of damage. Probably its worst damage, though, was to the weathermen's storm-research program.

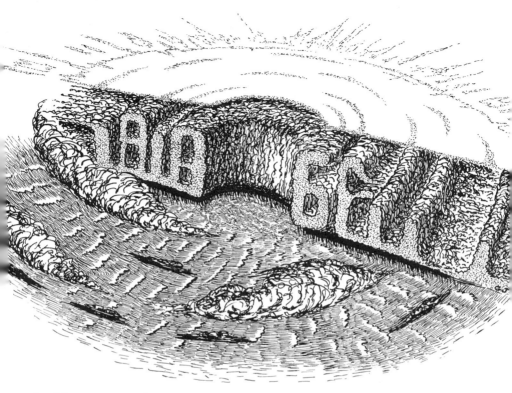

*In this cutaway of the cloud wall around the hurricane's eye (1), the black arrows indicate the points of low pressure where the ascending winds have found their easiest paths upward. The point of very lowest pressure (2) is now considered the hurricane's "primary energy cell," and the place where it may be most vulnerable to attack.*

There was a great outcry from everybody who had suffered from the storm, blaming the scientists for having "meddled" and made a disaster of a storm that otherwise wouldn't have done any damage. Actually, there was no way of proving that the seeding experiment had or had not affected the hurricane at all. Other storms had behaved more capriciously. But there was so much brouhaha about this one that the meteorologists hastily dropped all plans for any further such experiments—and it was fourteen years before they tried again.

Nevertheless, meteorologists did not stop studying the killer storms, trying to devise some safe and certain way of moderating their fury. In 1956, the National Hurricane Research Laboratory was set up at Miami. Hurricane Hunter planes continued to penetrate the storms; radar continued to track them; and, from 1960 on, the orbiting satellites watched them from space.

Some new facts about hurricanes began to emerge: for example, that the eye of the hurricane might not, after all, be its real central focus nor the place to attack the storm. True, the eye is the axis around which the winds spin, and from which the great pinwheel of cloud curls out. It is toward that eye that the inward and downward spiraling cool air is sucked; then it is upward through the cloud wall around the eye that the air rushes aloft, providing, as it does so, the energy that sustains the hurricane.

Now, however, Hurricane Hunter planes discovered that the eye is not always the storm's area of lowest air pressure. There might be as many as three other points within the cloud wall around it, as far as twenty miles apart, at which the pressure is lower. In other words, it seems to be at these specific points among the clouds that the skyward-rushing air somehow finds its easiest upward path, or pipe. No matter how many such points have been found in a storm's cloud wall, one of them is always lower in barometric pressure than the others. Of the several pipes up which the air is being sucked, *that* is the main one, the main connection between the sea-level inflow and the upper-atmosphere outflow of the storm system. The researchers named it the "primary energy cell" and decided that it might be the one spot at which a hurricane would be most vulnerable to attack.

Meanwhile, the U.S. Naval Weapons Center had developed an improved method of cloud seeding. Up to now, seeding had usually been done by an airplane dropping a sprinkle of silver iodide crystals, like a crop-duster plane spraying insecticide over a farm field. It was impractical to do that over the great cloud banks of a hurricane; the terrific winds would hold the chemical particles aloft, and not let them get down into the clouds where they could begin the process of crystallizing the water vapor.

What the Naval Weapons Center came up with was a silver iodide generator called the Alecto. A cylinder only eight inches long and weighing seven pounds, it was designed to be dropped into a cloud like a little bomb. As it plummeted downward, it spewed out a "smoke" of silver iodide. In forty seconds, it fell 20,000 feet,

*This composite photograph shows (center) an Alecto silver iodide generator and the results of dropping the iodide "seeds" into a cloudy patch of sky. At upper left is the cloud area immediately after the seeding; notice that one cloud in the middle of the picture has begun to bulge. Some of its water vapor has been crystallized into ice particles, thus releasing heat energy that creates a warm updraft and boosts the cloud top skyward. In the subsequent photographs (top right and lower left) the seeded cloud continues to grow. The ice crystals are collecting other droplets, getting heavier, releasing still more heat, and causing a stronger updraft. In the lower right photograph, the cloud has assumed the typical "anvil" shape of a thunderhead, and rain is pouring from its lower levels.*

*ESSA*

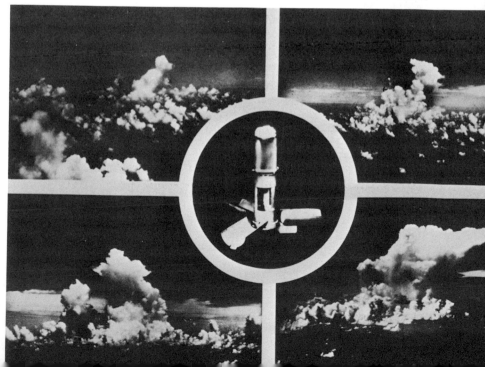

leaving the chemical particles suspended in the cloud all the way down behind it.

In 1961, a few Alectos were dropped into hurricane Esther. Immediately the small section of the cloud that had been seeded disappeared from a watching radarscope. Since the radar was of the type that detects clouds by bouncing radio echoes off their water droplets, *something* had happened to those droplets. Evidently the silver iodide had succeeded in crystallizing them into ice particles.

The result of that first hesitant Alecto experiment was encouraging enough that, in 1962, the U.S. Department of Commerce and the Department of Defense joined in organizing "Project Stormfury" to conduct further such tests. A year later, the Project dropped its Alecto seeds into part of the cloud wall of another hurricane, 1963's Beulah. The result was an increase in the barometric pressure of the eye (that is, the uprush of air through it had slowed) and the area of fiercest winds moved outward some distance from the storm's center.

But both of these experiments had been confined to such small portions of the storms, and so few Alectos had been dropped, that the results were inconclusive. The meteorologists could not be sure if the storms' subsequent changes had been their doing. So Project Stormfury asked the Government's permission to make an all-out full-scale Alecto attack on the primary energy cell of the next suitable hurricane that came along.

In 1965 Stormfury got that permission, but a severely restricted one. Government officials, remembering the disaster of that 1947 storm and the even stormier aftermath of public outrage, told Project Stormfury that it could conduct its experiments only in a limited area of the Atlantic, well out to sea, between Puerto Rico and Bermuda, from which no hurricane had ever turned west to strike the American mainland. On the average, less than one storm per year ever went through that narrow corridor.

Stormfury's weathermen and air crews waited through the 1965 hurricane season. Finally, in September, along came hurricane Betsy, headed right for the experiment area. Then, at the last minute, when the Hurricane Hunter seeding planes were literally warming up on their runways, Betsy turned away from the target area. Project Stormfury was disbanded for the year.

By now, the American people were aware of Stormfury's plans, but they were never notified that the Project had given up on Betsy. And, as described in Chapter 6, Betsy turned out to be the most vicious and destructive storm that has ever hit America in all of

*Aboard an ESSA Hurricane Hunter plane, Project Stormfury's director, Dr. R. Cecil Gentry (center, with glasses) leads some of his technicians through a "dry run" of the assault that was later carried out in reality against 1969's hurricane Debbie.*

*ESSA*

history. So there was another blast against the scientists' "meddling," this one even more angry and prolonged than that of 1947. Eventually a Congressional investigation had to be carried out, to satisfy the public that Betsy had not been tampered with, that the storm's abrupt change of course and the violence of its onslaught were nobody's fault.

In 1966, again, no hurricane passed through the limited Atlantic corridor allowed for Project Stormfury's planned operation. The Project's directors pointed out to the Government that it was wasting a lot of money, keeping a large staff of scientists and military men, and a fleet of aircraft, waiting and watching a patch of ocean through which a hurricane might never come.

The Government agreed and, for the 1967 season, extended the Project's experimental area so that almost any storm coming up through the Atlantic would be eligible for attack—with one proviso. The scientists of ESSA and the Weather Bureau would have to guarantee that the storm they selected had a less than 10 percent probability of approaching the populated coast within twenty-four hours after the experiment.

The Stormfury weathermen and airmen again waited out the peak weeks of the hurricane season. Now they had a vast area of ocean to watch, and they were certain that this year they would get their chance to try killing a killer storm. But, on October 16, Project Stormfury again disbanded in frustration. For the first time in fourteen years, not a single hurricane had made its way through that target area.

While waiting for a storm, the scientists and military men continued to study and devise improvements in their seeding techniques. They invented an improvement on the Alecto silver iodide generator. This new canister, called the Stormfury I, is smaller, more compact, and efficient. It is designed to emit just a dribble of its chemical "smoke" during the first part of its fall through the clouds, and then, after it is deep inside the hurricane, to let go the bulk of its iodide crystals from 20,000 feet down to 13,000, the area where they should have the most telling effect.

In 1968, Stormfury's operational area was still further extended, now taking in parts of the Caribbean Sea and the Gulf of Mexico. The Project's advisory panel had decided that these areas would also be safe for the experiment because by this time, with the help of new satellites and computers, the Weather Bureau's techniques of hurricane forecasting had improved so much that the Stormfury staff could be trusted to pick for their attack a fairly harmless hurricane. From early August to mid-October, the Project's personnel, newsmen, and other observers (including the author of this book) waited anxiously on a forty-eight hour standby alert, prepared to fly to the scene of operations the minute a suitable hurricane hove into view.

The 1968 season began promisingly. Three hurricanes appeared in the Caribbean and the Gulf in the month of June—only the fourth time in weather history that so many storms had appeared so early in the year—an indication that the season ought to bring plenty of opportunities for Stormfury's experiment. However, after the first salvo of storms, only three other hurricanes developed during the whole summer, and all of them stayed too far out at sea for the land-based planes to reach with ease. Stormfury's operational period again petered out in frustration. Once more the Project's people abandoned their storm watch, on October 15.

And then, *the very next day,* an unremarkable tropical storm in the Caribbean Sea suddenly intensified into a full-size hurricane, the seventh and last of the season, but the first that might have been suitable for the seeding attack. After crossing the western tip of Cuba on October 16, hurricane Gladys spent two days traversing what had been Stormfury's target zone in the Gulf of Mexico. On October 19, Gladys picked up speed and churned across the peninsula of Florida, killing three people, injuring many more, and doing several million dollars' worth of damage. In the following year, 1969, thirteen hurricanes developed in the Atlantic and Caribbean, from Anna in June to Martha in November. The third of them, Camille, will probably rank as the second worst hurricane ever to hit the United States. It might well have earned a different distinction, that of being the target of Project Stormfury's first all-out seeding attack, except that Camille's approach was a sneaky one. It came all the way from Africa, across the Atlantic, as nothing more than an atmospheric disturbance. Not until it was just off Cuba did the disturbance develop hurricane force, and by then it was too close to inhabited areas to be safely assaulted.

However, there was another hurricane trailing across the Atlantic in Camille's wake, and this one, Debbie, spent its whole life well out at sea, vulnerable to Stormfury's long-awaited experiment.

In the pre-dawn darkness of Monday, August 18, 1969, the first plane of Project Stormfury's armada of aircraft took off from Puerto Rico for its engagement with hurricane Debbie, 700 miles to the east of that island. Altogether, more than two hundred weather scientists plus thirteen airplanes and their crews took part in the assault. It was as complex and formidable as any wartime battle mission, but it progressed with perfect timing and coordination.

As planned, the first plane to approach the storm was a U.S. Navy Hurricane Hunter, a propeller-driven Super Constellation fitted with special radar and a complete flying laboratory staffed by Project meteorologists. The plane arrived in the storm area at 6:15 A.M., four hours before T-time—"T" meaning "Tango," the code word that would be radioed to signal the first drop of the silver iodide generators. This first plane's job was to circle hurricane Debbie at a very low altitude, measuring the sea-level inflow of winds fueling the storm.

An hour later, three hours before Tango, an ESSA B–57 jet,

converted from a bomber to a data-collecting Hurricane Hunter, arrived to start circling high above the storm, where it measured the outflow of Debbie's exhaust winds. At the same time, an ESSA DC-6 propeller plane and another Super Constellation started making flights back and forth directly through the storm's eye and cloud wall. The purpose of these flights was to locate the storm's primary energy cell and to decide on the best angles of attack.

Meanwhile, the Command Control plane—still another Super Constellation, carrying all of the Project's directors—took position far enough away from the hurricane that it wouldn't be bothered by turbulence, but near enough for the operation's commanders to keep the other planes in view, when possible, and to control and direct them by radio signals.

Shortly before T-time, a twin-jet A-6 Intruder bomber of the U.S. Navy moved into a holding pattern, circling high around the storm's top and fifty miles from its center. When all of the other planes' preliminary investigations had been completed, the pilot of the Intruder was told what path he was to fly and where he was to start his "bombing."

Finally, at 10:15 that morning, the code word "Tango!" was flashed from the Command Control plane across the miles of sky and storm. Immediately the Intruder broke out of its circular holding pattern and rammed through the winds of Debbie's cloud wall, dropping two hundred of the Stormfury I canisters at the rate of six per second along the predetermined track.

Every two hours thereafter—at Tango-plus-two-hours, Tango-plus-four, plus-six and plus-eight—another Intruder bomber arrived to make a fresh bombing run, each time dropping another two hundred generators along a particular stretch of the central cloud wall or the outward-spiraling rain band clouds. In all, the Intruder pilots made five runs and dropped a thousand silver iodide canisters.

In between these runs, one and then another of the monitor

planes returned to the Puerto Rico airfield to turn its records over to land-based Project scientists for instant analysis, while other planes took their places in the storm area to collect new data. For example, U.S. Air Force Hurricane Hunters, a prop-driven Hercules and a B–47 jet, circled around and probed into Debbie just to take photographs of the storm.

The last seeding was done at 6:15 that evening. For six more hours, Stormfury's monitor planes stayed with Debbie—maneuvering around its flanks, weaving in and out of its rain belts, plunging through its inner cloud walls, hovering inside its eye—while their airborne thermometers, barometers, hygrometers, anemometers, and other equipment made permanent records of every second-by-second aspect of the storm.

At fifteen minutes after midnight, Tango-plus-fourteen-hours, the experiment was over. The planes droned back to their home bases. The weathermen went back to their maps, slide-rules, radarscopes, and computers, to calculate what changes might already have occurred in the storm, and to wait for any further developments.

What was the result of Project Stormfury's assault on hurricane Debbie? Nothing, to judge from the news reports next day, but the newsmen didn't have the whole story. The first headlines said things like, *"No Change Seen in Seeded Storm,"* as if Debbie had been expected to disappear like a soap bubble pricked with a pin.

There *had* been a significant change in Debbie, and it *had* been seen, though not by human eyes peering down at it from the monitor planes, because the change had been in the make-up of the clouds, not in the look of them. As the seeding progressed, the men at the radarscopes saw large areas of Debbie's clouds fade and vanish from their screens. This was the same thing that had happened eight years earlier with the small-scale seeding of hurricane Esther, but now it happened to much vaster areas of hurricane Debbie. The seeding had again succeeded in crystallizing the storm clouds' water droplets into ice particles, and this time in far more immense quantities than in any previous experiment.

By rights, this should have caused another change in the hurricane that would have been visible to the newsmen. The sudden crystallization of the clouds' water into ice should have drained off some of the storm's energy and caused Debbie to get bigger in size but weaker in wind force. This did not happen, and at first the weather experts, too, were disappointed at their apparent failure to calm the storm's fury at least a little bit.

However, when the scientists sat down to make their first detailed examination of the mountains of data and measurements recorded during the experiment, they found out why the storm had not noticeably reacted. Unknown to them at the time, Debbie had actually begun to intensify in force on the very morning the Project's attack began. Thus any weakening effect that the seeding should have caused would have been canceled out in some degree by the storm's own build-up in strength at the time. The fact that Debbie merely persisted unchanged, not getting any tamer, but at least not getting any fiercer, seemed also to prove that the seeding had likewise canceled out the build-up.

Exactly how much the seeding affected the storm is hard for even the weathermen to estimate. Since this was the first time such an

*The attack and monitor planes of Project Stormfury stand poised on a Florida airfield, awaiting the arrival of a hurricane suitable for seeding in their assigned target area.*

*ESSA*

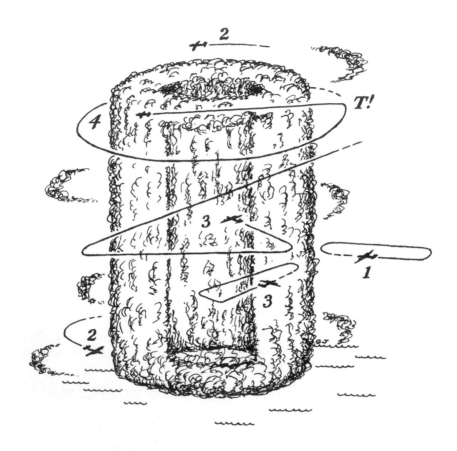

*Project Stormfury, August 18, 1969. While the Command Control plane (1) hovered at a distance from hurricane Debbie, monitor planes (2) circled the storm at high and low altitudes, and others (3) flew penetration patterns at intermediate levels. The attack bomber (4) idled around Debbie's crown until the signal "Tango!" was flashed, when it rammed through the cloud wall and started dropping its Stormfury I "seed" canisters. As the experiment progressed, other monitor planes arrived to circle, penetrate, or overfly the hurricane and measure the effectiveness of this first all-out assault on a killer storm.*

experiment had been tried on such a scale, nobody involved could have any precise idea of what to expect from it. Nobody can guess how much or how fast Debbie's force might have increased if it had been left alone. At this writing, the Stormfury scientists are still studying their figures, photographs, tape recordings, graphs, and computer print-outs. It may be months before all the data have been digested and conclusions drawn from them. Even then, considering all the unknown factors involved in a brand-new experiment and the incalculable forces at work in the hurricane, there are bound to remain a lot of unanswered questions and unresolved speculations.

Nevertheless, there is every reason to regard this first all-out experiment as a considerable achievement. For an initial venture it was, as one of the Project's directors described it, "meteorology's man on the moon." The seeding did produce a sufficient change in hurricane Debbie to encourage still more assaults on future storms. And the complex tactical operation of the actual seeding, coordinating so many men, instruments, and aircraft, went off without a hitch, indicating that similar task forces to be deployed against future storms can be depended upon to perform with the same brisk efficiency.

Project Stormfury will continue its experiments during future hurricane seasons, though the Project may, like the hurricanes, change its name from year to year. It will continue to learn from each new experiment, and each one should prove more successful. The experimenters may discover, for instance, that an effective seeding must consist of many more "bomb runs," and drop many more tons of silver iodide. Or they may learn exactly where to seed the hurricane's primary energy cell, or its rain belt clouds, or both. Or they may determine that a hurricane must be attacked at some particularly critical stage in its development. But we can be virtually certain that the weathermen will eventually achieve the ultimate and perfect experiment, and this is what will happen:

The silver iodide particles seeded into that hurricane will capture precisely the right amount of water droplets in the clouds and transform them into ice crystals. In this transformation, the droplets will release exactly the right amount of stored-up heat energy into the storm system around the primary energy cell. That is where the hurricane's fuel of cool air is rushing in and upward from around the storm's center, and the forced release of heat will warm that cool air prematurely. Its ordinarily high pressure will drop, nearer to the pressure level of the hot-air "pipe" that is sucking it in. Thus the inrush of air from outside will be forcibly slowed, and that will automatically slow the workings of the hurricane's whole energy engine.

The racing winds spiraling around the hurricane's eye will diminish, the tightly-coiled cloud wall will begin to loosen and expand. Meanwhile, the ice crystals created by the silver iodide will have attracted still more vapor to themselves, becoming heavy enough to fall as rain, thereby depriving the hurricane of still more of its store of energy.

The hurricane's winds will continue to fade, its forward movement will slow, the storm wave it is propelling across the ocean will begin to flatten and subside, the dense clouds will gradually thin out, and the once-mighty killer storm will degenerate into nothing more than a vast expanse of rain clouds. For the first time, man will have been able to strike back at the hurricane and stop it in its tracks.

As Project Stormfury indicated in 1969, man isn't likely to learn how to kill a killer storm in just one more year of experimenting, or five, or even twenty-five. No doubt different methods will have to be worked out for defense against different varieties of hurricanes and typhoons, depending on their size, intensity, forward speed and direction, the surrounding atmospheric and oceanic conditions, etc.

And probably man will never be able to ward off *every* hurricane that comes along. If one blows up too suddenly, moves too fast, and gets too near land before it can be seeded (as 1969's killer

Camille did), the seeding may be impossible. To force a hurricane to disgorge all of its tremendous energy in one torrential downpour of rain over a populated area would be rather like re-creating Noah's flood. It would wreak more havoc than would the un-molested hurricane.

Of the other killer storms, the tornado, too, is going to prove hard to tame. Essentially, any technique that can break down the energy engine of a hurricane should, with some variations, be able to do the same to a twister. The difficulty will be to get at it in time. A tornado appears so suddenly and strikes so fast that even a constantly patrolling fleet of planes, covering the whole sky, could hardly strike back at it before it does its damage. Our best hope is that improved forecasting techniques might enable the seeding and weakening of tornado-producing clouds well before the twister begins to twist.

But we can foresee that man will learn how to balk the hurricane, at least, and minimize its menace. When he does, what then? What will that mean to us?

It will mean that a large portion of mankind will no longer have to fear the weather through a large part of the year. It will mean that scores and hundreds of people now untimely doomed to die in each hurricane season will live out their lives to their natural extent. Vast acreages of crops now ruined each year will grow up to be harvested and will put more food on more tables at less cost. Homes and ships and factories and family cars and personal pos-sessions will no longer be demolished. New cities can grow in places where now they dare not, or where they are presently dis-couraged by impossible insurance rates. Great stretches of land now lying fallow and neglected can become fruitful with gardens and farms and ranches.

There are many ways, both great and small, in which man can hope to improve his planet. Unquestionably one of the greatest improvements will be to curb the killer storms. And this once-unimaginable achievement now seems well within his reach.

# INDEX